Advance Praise for

BLACKOUT

In *Blackout*, Richard Heinberg has made a major contribution
to the coal debate. What is new is his focus on the question of
how much minable coal there is. Governments have consistently
over-estimated it, but the answer is critical for climate policy
and for planning for alternative sources of electricity.

— David Rutledge, Tomiyasu Professor of Electrical Engineering
Former Chair, Division of Engineering and Applied Science
California Institute of Technology

Coal lies at the very center of our predicament as a
civilization — it's the habit we must kick, and fast, as
Richard Heinberg makes abundantly clear in this powerful
volume. It's your program for understanding the drama
now unfolding on the global stage.

— Bill McKibben, author *Deep Economy*

Blackout provides a startling wake-up call for energy
optimists who believe our economic future is guaranteed
by centuries worth of available coal — as well as for
environmentalists who see "peak coal" as a salvation from
climate hell. This clearly written and meticulously documented
book provides a powerful case for a rapid global program
to rewire the world with clean energy. Any other option
puts the survival of our coherent civilization at risk.

— Ross Gelbspan, author, *The Heat Is On* and *Boiling Point*

BLACKOUT

COAL, CLIMATE AND THE LAST ENERGY CRISIS

RICHARD HEINBERG

NEW SOCIETY PUBLISHERS

Cataloging in Publication Data:
A catalog record for this publication is available from the National Library of Canada.

Cover design: Diane McIntosh.
Cover images: Coal: ©iStock/ilbusca; Horizon: ©iStock/Clint Spencer

Printed in Canada.
First printing May 2009.

Paperback ISBN: 978-0-86571-656-8

Inquiries regarding requests to reprint all or part of *Blackout* should be addressed to New Society Publishers at the address below.

To order directly from the publishers, please call toll-free (North America) 1-800-567-6772, or order online at www.newsociety.com

Any other inquiries can be directed by mail to:

New Society Publishers
P.O. Box 189, Gabriola Island, BC V0R 1X0, Canada
(250) 247-9737

New Society Publishers' mission is to publish books that contribute in fundamental ways to building an ecologically sustainable and just society, and to do so with the least possible impact on the environment, in a manner that models this vision. We are committed to doing this not just through education, but through action. This book is one step toward ending global deforestation and climate change. It is printed on Forest Stewardship Council-certified acid-free paper that is **100% post-consumer recycled** (100% old growth forest-free), processed chlorine free, and printed with vegetable-based, low-VOC inks, with covers produced using FSC-certified stock. Additionally, New Society purchases carbon offsets based on an annual audit, operating with a carbon-neutral footprint. For further information, or to browse our full list of books and purchase securely, visit our website at: www.newsociety.com

NEW SOCIETY PUBLISHERS

Mixed Sources
Cert no. SW-COC-001271
© 1996 FSC

FSC

Contents

Acknowledgments

IN THE PREPARATION OF THIS BOOK I was aided immeasurably by Julian Darley, who read each of the chapters in draft form and provided many useful comments; Laura Rodman, whose research, fact-checking, and documentation were crucial; my colleagues Daniel Lerch and Asher Miller, at Post Carbon Institute, who participated in scenario discussions for Chapter 8; and David Rutledge, who offered key suggestions and corrections late in the writing process. And of course thanks, as always, to the editorial team at New Society, including Ingrid Witvoet and Judith and Chris Plant. Any remaining errors in this rather data-laden text are my sole responsibility.

Introduction

As oil prices climbed during 2007 and 2008, another and perhaps more serious energy crisis loomed — one largely unnoticed by most Americans and Europeans.

A hundred or more countries are suffering, some acutely, from shortages of electricity; and in many instances, these blackouts are due to the lack of what is supposed to be the world's most abundant fuel — coal.

China has idled 50 of its coal-fired power plants for lack of fuel, and growing power outages threaten to undermine that nation's economy.

India's hydropower from the Himalayas is drying up due to global warming, and, though the country is pushing for more wind and solar power, its rapidly rising demand for coal is exacerbating both climate change and international coal shortages.

Pakistan and Afghanistan, battlefronts in America's war on terrorism, are routinely plunged into darkness.

South Africa's mining industry is plagued by a lack of reliable electric power to run its coal, gold, and diamond mining industries. In the rest of sub-Saharan Africa, nearly two-thirds of countries experience frequent and extended electricity outages,[1] and many are looking for coal to supplement inadequate hydropower resources.

Great Britain experiences power shortfalls with ever-greater frequency, with analysts describing the nation's electricity-generating infrastructure as "crumbling" and "inadequate" for 21st-century use; the industry estimates

1

that it will need to spend £100 billion building a new generation of power stations — more than has ever been spent before on any similar project in the country's history.[2] The British coal industry, once the world's largest and the main supplier of power to the national grid, is now virtually gone, largely due to the depletion of the country's once-vast coal reserves.

Some nations that can afford high oil prices don't have sufficient electricity to run refineries. And even energy-rich countries like Venezuela and Iran are not immune, suffering from electrical blackouts even as they export oil.

In the United States, energy experts forecast more frequent grid outages in years ahead due to lack of generation capacity and an aging grid infrastructure in need of thorough overhaul. America's coal appears abundant — indeed, the domestic industry has begun exporting more coal recently due to high international demand and soaring prices — but the quality of the coal that is being produced from US mines is declining, so America gets less energy from the resource even though more is being dug from the Earth.

The world depends on coal for 40 percent of its electrical generation capacity (a greater share than comes from any other single source), and coal has seemed endless in supply; yet the average price of coal doubled during the two years from mid-2006 to mid-2008, and its availability in even the near future is questionable in some countries that use large amounts.

Part of the coal supply problem arose from added transport costs and reduced reliability resulting from tight oil supplies. But depletion of the world's highest-quality coal reserves also added to the delays, the soaring electricity prices, and the power outages.

These problems are already of crisis proportions in many nations, though for most Western energy consumers they constitute merely an occasional annoyance or a vague worry. But if current trends continue, the likely consequences are difficult to overstate. Unless the world adopts a very different energy paradigm — and soon — problems with coal and electricity supplies can only spread and worsen year by year until, some time in the next two to three decades, human civilization approaches a universal, final Blackout.

Why Care About Coal?

1. The Economy

If coal were of declining importance in the world's energy mix, the problems of depletion and declining availability would not be serious. Instead, however, coal is at the center of energy planning for many nations — especially the burgeoning Asian economies. Despite environmental concerns, coal is seeing the fastest percentage growth in usage worldwide of any of the principal fossil fuels, and the fastest growth, in terms of BTUs delivered, of any energy source.

This resurgence was mostly unanticipated.

Coal was the first fuel of the industrial age; it was the world's primary source of energy from the end of the 19th century (when it supplanted wood) until the middle of the 20th (when it was overtaken by oil). More recently, natural gas has substituted for coal to some extent in electricity generation, partly because of growing concerns about greenhouse gas emissions (coal is the most carbon-intensive common fuel, natural gas the least); meanwhile oil has become the globe's most important fuel largely because of its role in transport.

The historic pattern was thus for industrial societies to move from low-quality fuels (wood contains an average of 12 megajoules per kilogram [Mj/kg], and coal 14 to 32.5 Mj/kg) to higher-quality fuels (an average of 41.9 Mj/kg for oil and 53.6 for natural gas); from more-polluting to less-polluting fuels; and from solid fuels to a liquid fuel easily transported and therefore well suited to a system of global trade in energy resources.

During the 20th century, fuel switching yielded decisive economic and even geopolitical advantages. In 1912, Winston Churchill, as Lord of the Admiralty, famously retooled Britain's navy to burn oil rather than coal, thus helping ensure victory over Germany in World War I.[3] Throughout the second half of the century, the US economy became less energy intensive (measured as the amount of energy required to produce each dollar of GDP) largely by switching away from coal toward oil and gas. A diesel locomotive uses only one-fifth the energy that a coal-powered steam engine would consume pulling the same train; in addition, oil-burning systems generally need less attention and burn cleaner than coal-burning systems. As a result, oil and gas generate from 1.3 to 2.45 times more economic value per unit of energy than coal does.[4]

As nations learned to take advantage of physical and functional differences in fuels, and strained to get more economic bang for their energy buck, coal was nearly always in the position of being the older, less-efficient, less-desirable source.

In short, the widespread assumption only a decade ago was that coal's moment in the energy spotlight had ended. While remaining an important fuel for electricity production, coal was in many people's minds an artifact of the 19th and early 20th centuries — the era of steam-powered looms, majestic ocean liners, and smoke-spewing locomotives. Futurists in the 1980s and '90s assured us that, with the dawn of the information age, energy would soon become "de-carbonized" as nations shifted to cleaner energy sources and more concentrated fuels.

However, during the past five years, global production of crude oil has remained static, despite demand growth — especially from Asian economies. And there is every indication that worldwide petroleum production will begin its inexorable, inevitable decline beginning around 2010. This is the often-discussed phenomenon of Peak Oil (explained, for example, in my book, *The Oil Depletion Protocol* 5). In the quarter century from 1980 to 2005, world oil use grew at an average rate of roughly 1.5 percent annually. During most of this period, prices were low — usually in the range of US$10 to $20. However, in the three years following May 2005, the rate of extraction of conventional crude oil stalled, while prices rose to an astonishing $147 before falling back substantially due to the impact of the economic crisis that began in 2008. Many analysts believe that by 2015 oil production will be *declining* at an annual rate of over two percent per year and prices may be in the multiple hundreds of dollars per barrel. While more exploration prospects for conventional oil exist, they are mostly in geographically remote or politically sensitive areas; meanwhile, shortages of drilling rigs and trained personnel are adding significantly to delays in bringing new projects on line. Enormous quantities of non-conventional fossil fuels exist that could be turned into synthetic liquid fuels (the bitumen deposits of Alberta, the heavy oil of the Orinoco basin in Venezuela, and the marlstone or "shale oil" of Wyoming and Colorado); however, the rate at which these substances can be extracted and processed is constrained by physical and economic factors — such as the need for enormous quantities of fresh water and natural gas for processing.

World production of natural gas will likely peak somewhat later than that of oil; however, regional conventional natural gas supply constraints are already appearing, primarily in North America (the most intensive consumer of the resource), as well as in Russia and Europe. Because only a small proportion is traded globally in the form of liquefied natural gas

(LNG), this means it may not be possible to avert regional shortages by resorting to seaborne imports.

In the face of these constraints for oil, gas, and unconventional fossil fuels, coal by comparison appears suddenly attractive again. The industrial world has abundant experience with it, the technology for producing and using it is well developed, and there is purportedly an enormous amount of it waiting to be mined and burned. New technologies, such as integrated gasification combined cycle (IGCC) power plants and methods to capture and store carbon, promise to make coal cleaner (though not cheaper) to use. In addition, there is increasing interest in deploying methods to turn coal into a synthetic liquid fuel able to substitute for oil (we will explore each of these technologies in more detail in Chapter 7).

Since economic growth generally implies more energy consumption, it should come as no surprise that nearly all of the current world expansion in coal consumption has occurred in the nations with the highest rates of economic growth — principally, China and India, but also Vietnam, South Korea, and Japan.

The shift in the world's economic center of gravity away from the United States and toward the great population centers of East and South Asia is being widely heralded as the primary economic trend of the new millennium. In recent years, China's economy has grown at an annual rate of 7 to 11.5 percent (a 7 percent constant growth rate implies a doubling of size every ten years: thus after 20 years the entire economy is four times its previous size, and after a mere 30 years it is eight times its original magnitude; at 11.5 percent annual growth, this eight-fold expansion comes in just 20 years). According to most expectations, China's GDP will exceed US$10 trillion by the end of the current decade, and will surpass US$20 trillion by 2020, making China's national economy then the world's largest. India's economic growth rate was 8.4 percent in 2006 and 9.2 percent in 2007. Currently, India is the world's fourth largest national economy, but at recent rates of growth it could advance to third place within a decade (current rankings according to the CIA World Factbook [6]).

China currently obtains nearly 70 percent of its energy from coal and is the world's primary coal consumer, using nearly twice as much as the next country in line (the United States). The quantities are staggering: in 2007 alone, China added electrical generating capacity — nearly all of it coal-based — equal to the whole of France's or Britain's entire electricity grid. During 2007, China's installed electricity generating capacity grew 17 percent, reaching over 700 gigawatts, second only to the United States' 900+ gigawatts.

India is now the world's third-largest consumer of coal, which provides nearly two-thirds of the nation's commercial energy (compared to the world average of 26 percent).

It is entirely foreseeable that this enormous, rapid growth in coal consumption should entail an equally enormous environmental cost.

Why Care About Coal?
2. The Environment
If there were sound economic reasons for industrial societies to switch from coal to oil and gas during the 20th century, there were equally compelling environmental reasons.

Coal is the dirtiest of the conventional fossil fuels. Sulfur, mercury, and radioactive elements are released into the air when coal is burned and are difficult to capture at source. During the early phase of the Industrial Revolution, both the mining and the burning of coal generated legendary amounts of pollution. In cities like London, Chicago, and Pittsburgh, smoke and airborne soot reduced visibility to mere inches on some days. The following passage from *The Smoke of Great Cities* by David Stradling and Peter Thorsheim conveys the experience of the inhabitants of these coal towns:

> One visitor to Pittsburgh during a temperature inversion in 1868 described the city as "hell with the lid taken off," as he peered through a heavy, shifting blanket of smoke that hid everything but the bare flames of the coke furnaces that surrounded the town. During autumn and winter this smoke often mixed with fog to form an oily vapor, first called smog in the frequently afflicted London. In addition to darkening city skies, smoky chimneys deposited a fine layer of soot and sulfuric acid on every surface. "After a few days of dense fogs," one Londoner observed in 1894, "the leaves and blossoms of some plants fall off, the blossoms of others are crimped, [and] others turn black." In addition to harming flowers, trees, and food crops, air pollution disfigured and

eroded stone and iron monuments, buildings and bridges. Of greatest concern to many contemporaries, however, was the effect that smoke had on human health. Respiratory diseases, especially tuberculosis, bronchitis, pneumonia, and asthma, were serious public health problems in late-nineteenth-century Britain and the United States.[7]

The mining of coal was, in its early days, no less grim. Digging coal out of the ground is an inherently dangerous and environmentally ruinous activity, and accidents (from asphyxiation by accumulated gas, as well as from explosions, fires, and roof collapses) were so common as to be an expected part of life in mining towns. Miners and their families often suffered from respiratory ailments — including pneumoconiosis, or black lung disease. Mining altered landscapes, often resulting in polluted water and air, as well as the destruction of forests, streams, and farmland.

From the standpoint of safety, coal mining has cleaned up its act, at least in the more industrialized countries. The large-scale mechanization of mining means that today fewer miners are required to produce an equivalent amount of coal; meanwhile, improvements in mining methods (e.g., longwall mining), as well as hazardous gas monitoring (using electronic sensors), gas drainage, and ventilation have reduced the risks of rock falls, explosions, and unhealthy air quality. Even with these improvements, mining accidents still claimed 46 fatalities in the United States in 2006; according to the Bureau of Labor Statistics, mining remains America's second most dangerous occupation (logging is the first).[8]

However, despite technical advances, coal mining continues to destroy landscapes, as is infamously the case with the method used in the Appalachian region of the United States called "mountaintop removal." This practice, which involves clear-cutting native hardwood forests, using dynamite to blast away as much as 1,000 feet of mountaintop, and then dumping the waste into nearby valleys, often burying streams, has been called "one of the greatest environmental and human rights catastrophes in American history."[9] Families and communities near mining sites must contend with continual blasting from mining operations and suffer from airborne dust and debris. Floods have left hundreds dead and thousands homeless, and drinking water in many areas has been contaminated.

While the environmental and safety risks of both coal mining and coal consumption have been somewhat moderated in countries that industrialized early, in the nations where coal use is today the highest and is growing fastest, methods of mining and consumption often resemble the worst practices of the early 20th century.

Thousands of China's five million coal miners die from accidents each year (3,786 deaths were recorded in 2007). Meanwhile, acid rain falls on one-third of China's territory, and one-third of the urban population breathes heavily polluted air.[10] China's coal burning has put five of its cities in the top ten of the most polluted cities in the world, according to the International Energy Agency.[11]

Recently, very fine coal dust originating in China and containing arsenic and other toxic elements has been detected drifting around the globe in increasing amounts. In early April 2006, a dense cloud of coal dust and desert sand from northern China obscured nearby Seoul before sailing across the Pacific. Monitoring stations on the US West Coast found highly elevated levels of sulfur compounds, carbon, and other byproducts of coal combustion — microscopic particles that can work their way deep into the lungs, contributing to respiratory damage, heart disease, and cancer.

But as bad as all of these mostly longstanding environmental, health, and safety problems are, they pale in comparison to what many regard as the greatest crisis of our time — global climate change due to carbon dioxide emissions from the burning of fossil fuels. While coal produces a little over a quarter of the world's energy, it is responsible for nearly 40 percent of greenhouse gas emissions. Those emissions consist principally of carbon dioxide (CO_2), though coal mining also releases methane, which is 20 times as powerful a greenhouse gas as CO_2 and accounts for nine percent of greenhouse gas emissions created through human activity.

During the past decade, as a scientific consensus has solidified that global warming is due to human activity, the actual signs of climate change have often surpassed even the most dire forecasts. During the 2007 summer, Arctic sea ice reached a minimum extent of 4.13 million square kilometers, compared to the previous record low of 5.32 million square kilometers in 2005.[12] This represented a decline of 22 percent in just two years; the difference amounted to an expanse of ice roughly the size of Texas and California combined. Moreover, the average thickness of the ice has declined by about half since 2001. Altogether, taking into account both geographic extent and thickness, summer Arctic sea ice has lost more than 80 percent of its volume in four decades. At current rates of melting, the Arctic could be ice-free during summer months by 2013. While sea levels will not be directly affected by the total melting of the northern icecap, since it floats on and thus displaces ocean water, that event will severely destabilize Greenland's ice pack — whose disappearance would cause sea levels to rise by several meters, inundating coastal cities around the globe that are home to hundreds of millions of people.

Meanwhile, as deserts expand and climate zones shift, many species that are unable to move or adapt quickly enough find themselves on the precipice of extinction, and climate change-induced drought or changing monsoon patterns are sweeping every continent.

The crisis is being exacerbated by the fact that carbon sinks (forests and oceans that soak up carbon dioxide from the atmosphere) are losing their capacity. The net carbon uptake of northern forests is declining in response to autumnal warming. And evidence suggests that the oceans' ability to take up atmospheric carbon is also slowing, and perhaps even reversing.[13]

Meanwhile, the seas are acidifying as levels of carbonic acid — produced by the reaction of water with carbon dioxide — are increasing at a rate a hundred times faster than the world has seen for millions of years. The oceans are naturally alkaline but, since the Industrial Revolution, sea surfaces have grown increasingly acidic. Many millennia will pass before natural processes can return the oceans to their pre-industrial state. The sea life expected to be worst hit include organisms that produce calcium carbonate shells — including corals, crustaceans, mollusks, and certain plankton species. Larger sea fauna such as penguins and cetaceans will not be directly affected, but changes to the rest of the food chain will eventually impact these larger animals as well (see the section, "Climate Sensitivity" in Chapter 6).

From the human standpoint, the potential consequences of climate change for agriculture are particularly worrisome. According to the UN's World Food Program (WFP), 57 countries — including 29 in Africa, 19 in Asia, and 9 in Latin America — have been hit by catastrophic floods during the past few years. Harvests have been affected by drought and heat waves in South Asia, Europe, China, Sudan, Mozambique, and Uruguay. In 2007, the Australian government said that drought had slashed predictions for the coming winter harvest by nearly 40 percent, or four million tons.[14]

Altogether, human-induced climate change constitutes environmental impact on a scale never witnessed during the period of human civilization — i.e., the past 10,000 years.

Because coal produces higher carbon emissions per BTU of energy yielded than does oil or gas, as these other fossil fuels deplete and become more scarce and expensive, and as higher-quality coal depletes and nations turn to lower-quality coals, the climate situation will only grow worse — unless other sources of energy are developed quickly, or unless total energy use declines.

Efforts to capture carbon at power plants and sequester it in deep geological deposits could theoretically reduce the environmental burden from coal consumption, but there are snags and tradeoffs to that solution, as we will see in Chapter 7.

There is currently an enormous push underway to develop a global agreement to reduce greenhouse gas emissions, using cap-and-trade mechanisms to ration rights to emit carbon. This may turn out to be the most significant global policy discussion in world history, and it will have enormous implications for, among other things, the problem of global economic inequity — since national levels of per-capita energy consumption correlate closely with per-capita GDP.

Such a policy could also significantly impact the development of coal industries worldwide, and entire national economies that depend on coal.

But if size of the coal resource base is smaller than is generally believed, this would have enormous implications for climate science, economic planning, and government policy.

▦ ▦ ▦

In short: two of the defining trends of the emerging century — the development of the Asian economies and climate change — both center on coal. But coal is a finite, non-renewable resource. Thus, a discussion of the future of coal must also intersect with a third great trend of the new century: resource depletion.

These three great trends must inevitably interact and coalesce. How will this occur? Can current trends in coal consumption be sustained? If not, what does this mean for the global economy and for the environment? If such trends *cannot* be sustained, how *will* our energy future unfold?

These are, of course, enormously complex problems with vast implications — which we will unpack during the course of this book.

In Chapter 1, we will examine *how* coal supplies are estimated, and *why* new studies are challenging longstanding assumptions of abundance. As we will learn, estimating coal reserves is a complex task, and in many cases published figures are highly misleading.

Then in the four following chapters we will look in some detail at coal reserves in the United States, China, and the rest of the world, seeing why global supply shortfalls are likely within a mere two decades — in some nations, within just a few years; while in still others, coal supplies are already in trouble.

In Chapter 6 we will examine the implications of this new information for our understanding of the crisis of climate change.

Chapter 7 explores technologies that the coal industry is counting on to increase production and electricity generation efficiency, and to reduce carbon emissions.

Fig. 1

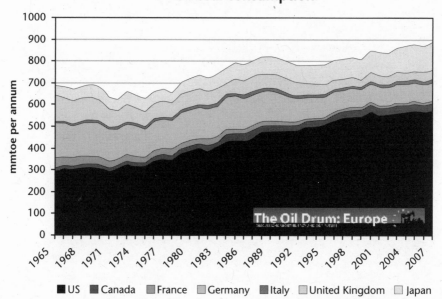

G7 coal consumption

■ US ■ Canada ■ France □ Germany ■ Italy □ United Kingdom □ Japan

Finally, in Chapter 8 we will examine three scenarios for the future, hinging on how much coal is consumed and whether the carbon from coal is captured and stored.

We begin with a rudimentary and somewhat technical question upon which our energy future, with all its economic and environmental implications, may ultimately pivot: *How do we know* how much coal we have?

CHAPTER 1

How Much Coal Do We Have?

"It has been estimated that there are over 984 billion tonnes of proven coal reserves worldwide. ...This means that there is enough coal to last us over 190 years."

— The Coal Resource, *World Coal Institute, 2005*

THE FIRST SCIENTIFIC FORECAST FOR FUTURE BRITISH COAL SUPPLIES, published by Edward Hull in 1864, promised a 900-year abundance.[1] Subsequent estimates stayed above 500 years for about a century. By 1984, the official forecast for British coal was down to 90 years' supply. As of 2008, Britain's coal industry, once the world's largest, is virtually gone.

The first scientific survey of US coal supplies, undertaken by the US Geological Survey in 1907, concluded that the nation had 5,000 years' worth of coal. Today, the US Department of Energy says that the country has a 200-year supply.

Somehow Britons evidently misplaced about 750 years' worth of coal, while Americans lost a staggering 4,700 years' worth. What happened?

Future supplies of coal are often discussed in terms of the reserves-to-production (R/P) ratio — i.e., the resource base estimated to be recoverable at current prices and with current technology, expressed in terms of annual consumption. This ratio is frequently stated as if it were a forecast of supply over time, as in, "the world has 190 years' worth of coal at current rates of consumption," or "China has a 100-year supply."

13

This sounds both reassuring and reasonable — simply a matter of common sense, easily illustrated with a homely metaphor to which we will return several times in the following paragraphs.

Imagine that you were in the habit of eating a can of soup for lunch every day and you looked in your cupboard and counted ten cans. You would correctly conclude that your daily reserves-to-consumption ratio for canned soup was 10/1, and that you have ten days' worth of soup.

It makes perfect sense. Why shouldn't the situation be similar for coal?

In fact, supply forecasts for nonrenewable natural resources based on R/P ratios are *always wrong,* and often dramatically so. This may seem like an unreasonably sweeping statement (surely such forecasts are correct at least once in a while?), but the evidence is clear: for practical purposes, real experience *never* conforms to forecasts based on R/P ratios.

There are three main reasons for this.

1. *Rates of consumption for energy and materials are never constant.* In most cases, as populations increase and economies expand, consumption continually grows. Let us say that demand for a given mineral is growing at 3.5 percent per year; in that case, a resource base that would have lasted 100 years at an initial, constant rate of consumption would be exhausted in only about half that time.

   In our canned-soup example above, the initial ten-day supply forecast will be dashed if your soup-loving brother shows up to stay for a week, and will have to be scaled back even further when your sister from Florida drops by for a few days, with her hungry teenage son in tow.

2. *It is physically impossible to maintain a constant or growing rate of extraction of any non-renewable resource until the moment when the resource is exhausted.* In the real world, time-based extraction profiles for non-renewable resources tend to conform to a modified bell curve. Extraction starts slowly, increases as demand grows and exploration efforts expand, reaches a peak when the most easily-accessed portion of the resource has been depleted, and declines gradually thereafter as only the more remote and lower-quality deposits are able to be found and produced.

   Again, back to our example: Suppose your soup cans aren't stacked nicely in the cupboard, but have been randomly concealed around the house by a deranged former housekeeper, some in plain sight and others hidden in walls and under floor boards (this more closely resembles the actual situation with non-renewable natural resources, which must be located through prospecting efforts). You will find the cans that are in plain sight right away and exhaust them fairly quickly; after your brother has shown up and the two of you have polished off those first few, you may have to spend considerable time and effort taking the house apart, combing the wreckage for more. Perhaps many days or even weeks later, after your famished sister and nephew have joined in the search, will you discover the last can.

3. *Reserves are not static, but can increase as a result of new discoveries, higher prices (which make lower-quality deposits more attractive), and new technologies that facilitate exploration and production.* Our soup metaphor has so far assumed a fixed supply, but in reality you are unlikely to be confined solely to the food stocks you have in your house at any given time. Instead, you will periodically go to the supermarket to buy more. If you have a car or even a bicycle, you can get there more easily, and also carry home larger quantities.

Obviously, the first two mitigating factors work to make the initial R/P forecast too optimistic, while the third trends in the other direction. Which factor carries the most weight? In the practical experience of resource extraction industries, the answer is rarely simple. Much depends, for example, on how fast demand is growing, or on how much of the resource remains to be discovered. It is on this latter point that our canned-soup metaphor breaks down: when it comes to non-renewable resources, there is no supermarket with groaning shelves being regularly replenished from trucks, canneries, and farms; instead, there are finite quantities endowed by nature. As a result, one thing is certain — the third factor can only overcome the first two for a limited time; unless demand is rapidly *declining*, the resource will run out.

A low-hanging-fruit syndrome constrains both the discovery and production of most non-renewable resources. Deposits of minerals are continually being found; but, as exploration history lengthens, the tendency is to find only minor deposits that were missed the first time around. Meanwhile, production continues to grow, perhaps for decades, until (as we have already noted) the difficulties of recovering the remaining resource force a peak and subsequent decline in extraction rates.

With energy resources, production ultimately must cease when the amount of energy required to produce the resource equals the energy content of the resource being produced.

Some of the resource will always be left in the ground — and this often amounts to a majority of what was originally in place.

Therefore the world's coal reserves will not last 190 years. In fact, they will last much longer, as there will surely still be some recoverable coal left many centuries from now. But that truism actually tells us nothing useful. For economic planning purposes, what is far more useful to know is *the timing of the point when it will no longer be possible to increase yearly production rates.* The shape of the depletion profile is far more informative than the R/P ratio.

It may be helpful to consider a couple of examples in order to gain some understanding of just how misleading R/P forecasts can be.

During the 1970s, exploration geologists identified enormous oil deposits under British-controlled regions of the North Sea. As discoveries accumulated, reserves grew. With low initial production, the R/P ratio was high. As production ramped up, the largest fields that had been found early on gradually became depleted. By 1999, it was no longer possible to increase the aggregate rate of extraction, and British oil production began to falter. By 2008, total production from all fields combined had declined to about half its peak level. But paradoxically, because reserves figures have remained fairly constant (since some discoveries are still taking place in the North Sea while production is falling), R/P ratios have actually *increased* in recent years. If one were looking to the oil R/P ratio as the main index of the health of Britain's petroleum economy, this could only be encouraging. Yet Britain has recently been forced to become a net oil importer for the first time in 30 years.

For the past 25 years, the R/P ratio for oil produced in the United States has been between 9 and 12 years. On one hand, this seems cause for worry, if it means that America could run out of oil in only a decade; on the other hand, the fact that the ratio hasn't changed in a quarter-century is encouraging, because it implies that reserves are being constantly replenished. However, that appearance of replenishment is itself misleading, because it is mostly due to America's extremely conservative oil reserves reporting rules. Meanwhile, US oil production has generally been declining since 1970, and the nation — which was formerly the

Net Energy

Net energy is the amount of useful energy delivered to society from energy-harvesting efforts, after all energy expenditures associated with those efforts have been subtracted.[2] This is sometimes expressed as the ratio of energy returned on energy invested (EROEI). Society depends upon maintenance of a positive net energy balance. However, energy harvesting from non-renewable sources is subject to the law of diminishing returns, such that EROEI tends to decline as the resource is depleted. Fossil fuels in place become useless as energy sources when the energy required to extract them equals or exceeds the energy that can be derived from burning them. This fact puts a physical limit to the portion of resources of coal (or oil or gas) that should be categorized as reserves.

The graph shows a theoretical depletable resource that follows the "best first" (or "low-hanging fruit") policy of resource extraction. The vertical axis is quantity and the horizontal is time. The gross energy resource "X" is the entire area under the curve ("X" = "A"+ "B"+ "C"+ "D"). Direct energy costs are "D." Indirect energy costs (like tractors and highways and medical insurance and such) are "C." Environmental externalities (in energy terms) are "B." "A" represents the total net energy of the resource after costs have been subtracted. At any given point in time the energy returned on energy invested (EROEI) can be calculated by taking a ratio of the total area divided by the costs (depending on the boundaries). As can be seen, net energy peaks and goes to zero long before the total gross energy is depleted.

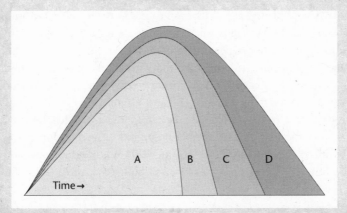

Fig. 2

world's petroleum powerhouse — now imports two-thirds of its oil. In other words, there is little or no useful correspondence between what has been happening with oil reserves and R/P ratios for the United States and what has been happening with actual production.

From all of this it seems fair to conclude that, as a tool for forecasting future supplies of nonrenewable resources such as coal or oil, the R/P ratio is utterly worthless. We use it to try (always unsuccessfully!) to answer the wrong question — *When will reserves be exhausted?*, when what we really need to know is, *When will the rate of production begin to decline despite continuing efforts to increase it?* Nevertheless, official agencies such as the Energy Information Administration of the US Department of Energy still prominently list current world and national coal R/P ratios, while making no effort to forecast peaks of production.[3]

Part of the appeal of the R/P ratio is its simplicity. However, the real world is complicated. With regard to coal, part of that complexity has to do with the extremely variable nature and quality of the resource. So any serious attempt to grasp the future supply situation must begin with an effort to incorporate that variability.

What Kind of Coal?

Coal is a fossil fuel and therefore non-renewable. A combustible, sedimentary, organic rock composed mainly of carbon, hydrogen, and oxygen, it was formed from vegetation consolidated between other rock strata and altered by the combined effects of pressure and heat over millions of years.

While oil and gas were formed primarily from enormous quantities of microscopic plants (algae) that fell to the bottoms of prehistoric seas, coal is the altered remains of ancient vegetation that accumulated in swamps and peat bogs (peat currently covers three percent of Earth's surface; in previous geologic eras, that percentage was much higher). While oil and gas were formed during two relatively brief periods of intense global warming roughly 150 and 90 million years ago, coal formation started much earlier and occurred during much longer time spans, with the first primary formation period occurring during the late Carboniferous period (roughly 360 to 290 million years ago), another in the Jurassic-Cretaceous (200 to 65 million years ago), and a third in the Tertiary (65 to 2 million years ago).

All fossil fuels vary in quality. For example, oil from some geological sources is more viscous and may have more impurities as compared to oil from other sources. Natural gas likewise varies by chemical composition: its main ingredient, methane, may be accompanied by larger or smaller amounts of sulfur dioxide, hydrogen sulfide, carbon dioxide, or other impurities; if the latter are present in too great a degree the gas is considered uncommercial and is not extracted.

Coal's variability is in some respects even greater than that of oil or gas: the range of energy density between and among hard and soft coals is wide, as is the range of impurities in coals from differing regions. (Much of this variability has to do with the degree of alteration undergone by the original plant material, a process known as *coalification*.) At the high end of the coal spectrum is anthracite — a hard, black coal that has more carbon, less moisture, and produces more energy per kilogram than other coals. At the low end are lignite and subbituminous coals, which are brown, friable, and have more moisture, less carbon, and a lower energy content. Again, coal that contains high amounts of mineral impurities (especially sulfur) may be unusable.

The qualities of coal determine its uses. Generally, only anthracites and some high-carbon bituminous coals are suitable for making coke for steel production, a process that requires high temperatures; these are therefore often referred to as "metallurgical coals" or "coking coals." Since anthracite is much less abundant than other coals, it sells for higher prices; it also therefore tends to be mined preferentially. Other coals are used mainly for electricity generation and are therefore known as "steam coals," but this category includes a wide variety of coal types, from bituminous to lignite. At the lowest end of the spectrum are coals that are barely distinguishable from peat.

Even a thick seam of high-quality coal may be unrecoverable if it happens to lie beneath a town, school, or cemetery. Accessibility is also an important factor: lack of nearby transport infrastructure can pose a serious economic hurdle, since the transportation of coal can account for over 70 percent of its delivered cost.[4] The cheapest mode of transport for coal is by water; thus, coalfields nearest coastal areas are most likely to be tapped for the global export market. While the oil industry has learned to access offshore petroleum and gas, coal that is buried in marine environments is difficult to extract economically with current technology, although there are instances where this is done (undersea coal has been mined in Britain since the 18th century, and is currently mined also in Chile, Japan, China, and Canada).

The location of coal varies greatly in depth, from surface outcrops to seams buried thousands of feet down. In most instances, underground mining is practical only to a depth of about 3,000 feet (1,000 meters), although the world's deepest coal mine, in England, reaches 5,000 feet (1,500 meters). Obviously, the costs of mining at great depth are much higher than those of working at the surface, and the danger to miners increases as well. Worldwide, 40 percent of produced coal is surface mined (in the United States, about 60 percent of produced coal is surface mined).

Coal seams also vary in thickness, from only a few inches to well over 100 feet. Unless they are very close to the surface, seams less than 28 inches in thickness are likely to be uneconomic to mine.

These variations in energy density, quality, location, depth, and thickness all must figure into calculations when geologists and energy analysts attempt to answer the question, "How much useful coal exists?" Cut-off points for whether coal is judged economical to produce tend to be vague and changeable. Two variables capable of affecting such decisions are price and technology. If the price of coal rises, producers may find it economical to dig deeper, to exploit thinner seams, or to mine lower-quality deposits. And with new machines for mining, coal that was uneconomic to extract in the past may become profitable.

Total world reserves (at end of 2002):	
bituminous coal + anthracite	479 billion tons
subbituminous coal	272 billion tons
lignite	158 billion tons
Each coal class has a different energy content:	
anthracite	30 MJ/kg
bituminous coal	18.8-29.3 MJ/kg
subbitiminous coal	8.3-25 MJ/kg
lignite	5.5-14.3 MJ/kg
wood	12 MJ/kg
coal	14-32.5 Mj/kg
oil	41.9 Mj/kg
natural gas	53.6 MJ/kg

On one hand, as more coal is discovered, as the price goes up, or as new mining machines are developed, coal reserves expand. On the other hand, as we extract and use enormous amounts of coal each year, we draw down those reserves.

One might expect that overall reserves figures would change fairly slowly and in a predictable fashion. In fact, as we will see, reserves figures for several nations have collapsed in recent years; and, over the past few decades, centuries' worth of coal has disappeared from global reserves. Given that the world's economy depends so heavily on coal, this trend is hardly reassuring. If we wish to understand how and why such downward reserves revisions are happening, it is essential that we look more deeply into the rather specialized, technical process of estimating coal reserves.

How Are Coal Reserves Estimated?

The estimation of coal reserves has evolved through the decades, and it now constitutes a sophisticated process entailing the work of thousands of trained and experienced coal geologists around the world.

The first step is to identify prospective areas. This is accomplished by means of old-fashioned, painstaking geological fieldwork, carried out with map, compass, and pick. Geologists typically look for coal outcroppings in rock strata exposed by streambeds or by ancient earth movements. Once a prospective area has been identified, cores are drilled to determine the thickness and depth of coal seams, as well as the quality and characteristics of the coal itself. These cores are carefully analyzed and logged to yield a three-dimensional map of the region. Then, using such maps, field sizes are estimated. Finally, reserves for entire regions are estimated by totaling field-by-field estimates.

No matter how carefully this process is pursued, it inevitably incorporates many judgment calls. Remember: reserves are defined not as the total amount of coal present (that's the *resource*); rather, they consist of the portion of the resource that can be expected to be extractable at a profit using existing technology. Not only are reserves limited by resource quality, seam thickness, depth, and location, but analysts must also take into account the fact that the mining process will inevitably leave some of the resource behind. This is especially true in the case of underground mining, where in some instances a majority of the coal originally in place is left behind.[5] Historically, practical recovery percentages for underground mining average about 50 percent of the coal that meets all economic criteria for minability; for surface mining, it is 85 percent.[6]

In the ideal case, all of these variables will have been taken into account when a final reserves number for a region or a nation is produced and published. However, ideal cases are rare.

The task of reserves analysts is made difficult, for example, by the fact that private coal companies often keep their data proprietary. Thus, when a public agency sets out to compile national reserves statistics, it may find significant gaps in available data. Moreover, some nations simply don't have the personnel or funding needed in order to properly compile and update records.

Additionally, there is no single internationally recognized, uniform method for assessing and reporting reserves as a fraction of resources. In the United States, coal geologists work with the following carefully defined categories:

original resources	inferred reserves
remaining resources	indicated reserves
identified resources	measured reserves
inferred resources	marginal reserves, and
measured resources	sub-economic resources.[7]
reserve base	

But other countries have their own sets of categories, with varying definitions. Assembling national reserves figures into a composite global picture is therefore a task of enormous complexity. One might expect that this would be the work of teams of data analysts working for the International Energy Agency (IEA) or some well-funded, prestigious institute. Surprisingly, the task is actually carried out by a two-person team — Alan Clarke and Judy Trinnaman, whose company, Energy Data Associates, is headquartered in Dorset, England. Clarke and Trinnaman send a questionnaire every three years to every coal-producing nation in the world. According to Clarke, about two-thirds of nations reply, but only about 50 of these replies typically are useful. Some reported data must simply be disregarded as unrealistic. No effort is made to verify reported national reserves figures through independent geological surveys.[8]

The figures from Energy Data Associates are then taken up in the triennial report of the World Energy Council, and are subsequently republished by the IEA, US Geological Survey, BP, etc.

Clarke and Trinnaman no doubt do an excellent service with the information available to them, but given the nature of this data the results can hardly be regarded with a high level of confidence.

Recent Studies of Coal Reserves and Future Supplies

As underscored in the Introduction, questions regarding future world coal supplies are not just academic. The global economy is more reliant on coal today than at any time in the past as total production is at the highest level in history. Meanwhile, the questions of how and whether the world continues its coal consumption are crucial to the fate of the global climate. Accurate coal reserves figures and supply forecasts are therefore more important than ever, as the world plans its energy strategy for the remainder of this century.

The common assumption that the world has plenty of coal has been the subject of several recent studies. Five of the most important of these will be summarized below, and we will return to them in the next four chapters as we examine the status of coal reserves and production in the world's main coal countries. These studies do not all reach the same conclusions, but they represent the best, most recent data and analysis available.

1

"Coal: Resources and Future Production" (Energy Watch Group). The organization Energy Watch Group (EWG) was founded by German parliamentarian Hans-Josef Fell, and is supported by the Ludwig-Bölkow-Foundation. Its mission is to assess future supplies of fossil and atomic energy resources, and develop scenarios for renewable energy sources and strategies for a long-term secure energy supply at affordable prices. The EWG report, "Coal: Resources and Future Production," was released in March 2007.[9] Its central conclusions are that minable global coal reserves are much smaller than is commonly thought, and that a peak in world coal production is likely within only ten to 15 years.

The report's authors — Werner Zittel (Ludwig-Bölkow-Systemtechnik GmbH, Ottobrunn) and Jörg Schindler (Managing Director, Ludwig-Bölkow-Systemtechnik GmbH) — state their opinion that "the data quality [for coal reserves] is very unreliable," especially for China, South Asia, and the former Soviet Union countries. Some nations (such as Vietnam) have not updated their "proved reserves" for decades, in some instances not since the 1960s. China's last update was in 1992; since then, 20 percent of its reserves have been consumed, though this is not revealed in official figures.

Even more striking is the fact that since 1986, all nations with significant coal resources (excepting India and Australia) that have made efforts to update their reserves estimates have reported *substantial downward revisions*. (In its 2007 survey, the World Energy Council noted that India reduced its reserves from 92Gt to 56Gt; this survey was published after the EWG report.) Some countries — including Botswana, Germany, and the United Kingdom — have downgraded their reserves by more than 90 percent. Poland's reserves are now 50 percent smaller than was the case 20 years ago. Each new assessment (again, except in the cases of India and Australia) has followed the general trend. These downgrades cannot be explained by the volumes of coal produced in this period. The best explanation, according to EWG, is that nations now have better data from more thorough surveys. If that is the case, then future downward revisions are likely from countries that continue to rely on decades-old reserves estimates.

Fig. 3

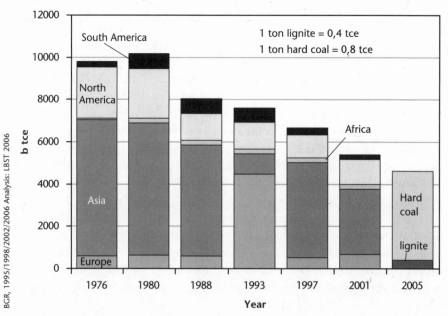

History of assessment of world coal resources

BGR, 1995/1998/2002/2006 Analysis: LBST 2006

Worldwide possible coal production

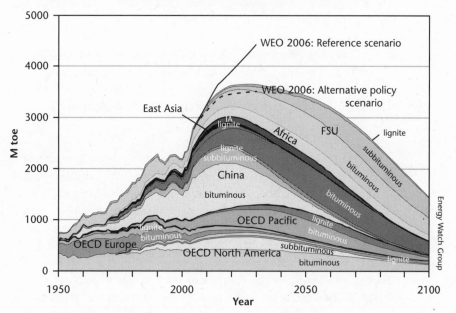

Fig. 4

The report concludes: "present and past experience does not support the common argument that reserves are increasing over time as new areas are explored and prices rise." This conclusion is supported by the fact that even the world's in-situ resources of coal have dwindled from 10 trillion tons of hard coal equivalent (hce) in 1980 to 4.2 trillion tons in 2005 — a 60 percent downward revision in 25 years.

The EWG group performed a peaking analysis of world coal, and arrived at the conclusion that world production will reach a maximum level around 2025, decline slowly for about two decades, and then fall off more rapidly beginning around 2050.

2

"A Supply-Driven Forecast for the Future Global Coal Production" (Höök, Zittel, Schindler, Aleklett; Uppsala Hydrocarbon Depletion Study Group). Two of the authors of this 2008 report were also responsible for the EWG study, so it might be expected that the conclusions of both would be similar — and this is indeed the case. However, the newer report is also somewhat more thorough. Future global coal production is forecasted using a logistic growth model, as well as experience from historical reserve and resource assessments. The result is the same:

> Global coal production will be able to increase over the next 10 to 15 years by about 30%, mainly driven by China, India, Australia and South Africa. A plateau will be reached around 2020 and the global production will go into decline after 2050.[10]

The authors again show that throughout the past century both reserves and resources have been constantly downgraded in most nations. Competition from other energy sources and the introduction of various political restrictions were involved in these downward reductions, but a main driver of the trend has been better geological understanding of actual available coal amounts.

It is pointed out that optimistic forecasts of future supply — see the BGR report, below — rely on the potential of new technology to turn resources (coal in the ground) into reserves (coal that we believe can be economically extracted). The authors note that, during the past century, the introduction of new technology for exploration and mining has had very little impact on the available coal reserves. They assume that this situation will continue:

> [T]he world's future coal supply likely is overestimated, as the entire concept of having resources upgraded to reserves needs to be reassessed, since it is something that has not happened throughout history on a significant scale. More careful studies of this need to be undertaken and all details in the mechanism of resource upgrading should be examined to find a suitable behaviour for future production forecasts.[11]

The authors note that, "Throughout history resources have not mattered much, and unless something causes a significant deviation in the historical trend, they will not matter much in the future." They call for "better data and a more transparent and reliable system for reserve evaluations" in order "to form a solid basis for long-term decisions and forecasts regarding the energy system."

3

"The Future of Coal." This study, by B. Kavalov and S.D. Peteves of the Institute for Energy (IFE), prepared for the European Commission Joint Research Centre and published February 2007, questions future supply, but does not attempt a peaking analysis.

While Kavalov and Peteves discuss future supply in terms of the familiar but misleading reserves-to-production (R/P) ratio, nevertheless, the IFE's conclusions broadly confirm those of EWG.

The three primary take-away conclusions from this study are as follows:[12]

- "World proven reserves (i.e., the reserves that are economically recoverable at current economic and operating conditions) of coal are decreasing fast ... ."
- "The bulk of coal production and exports is getting concentrated within a few countries and market players, which creates the risk of market imperfections."
- "Coal production costs are steadily rising all over the world, due to the need to develop new fields, increasingly difficult geological conditions and additional infrastructure costs associated with the exploitation of new fields."

Early in the paper the authors ask, "Will coal be a fuel of the future?" Their disturbing conclusion, many pages later, is that "coal might not be so abundant, widely available and reliable as an energy source in the future." Along the way, they state "the world could run out of economically recoverable (at *current* economic and operating conditions) reserves of coal much earlier than widely anticipated." The authors also highlight problems noted in the EWG study having to do with differing grades of coal and the likelihood of supply problems arising first with the highest-grade ores.

All of this translates to higher coal prices in coming years. The conclusion is repeated throughout the IFE report:[13] "[I]t is true that historically coal has been cheaper than oil and gas on an energy content basis. This may change, however. ... The regional and country overview in the preceding chapter has revealed that coal recovery in most countries will incur higher production costs in [the] future. Since international coal prices are still linked to production costs ... an increase in the global price levels of coal can be expected."

As prices for coal rise, "the relative gap between coal prices and oil and gas prices will most likely narrow," with the result that "the future world oil, gas, and coal markets will most likely become increasingly inter-related and the energy market will tend to develop into a global market of hydrocarbons."

4

Hubbert linearization and curve-fitting (studies by David Rutledge,[14] Jean Laherrère,[15] et al.). In the early 1980s, geophysicist M. King Hubbert (1900-1989) — who is generally credited with having pioneered the scientific study of oil depletion — developed a mathematical technique for forecasting ultimately recoverable figures for oil and the timing of production peaks using only production statistics. There are some who think that this technique can also be used to forecast future coal supplies.

Hubbert introduced the methodology, now known as "Hubbert linearization" (HL), in a paper titled "Techniques of Prediction as Applied to the Production of Oil and Gas," published in 1982.[16] It was later explained in some detail by Kenneth Deffeyes in his book *Beyond Oil: The View from Hubbert's Peak*.[17]

The assumption inherent in HL is that the ability to produce a non-renewable resource depends entirely, and linearly, upon the unproduced fraction of the recoverable resource at any point in time. Simply put, this is a mathematical way of modeling the fact that we tend to find and produce the most accessible portion of the resource first, so that production requires more effort over time.

Cumulative production is logged on the horizontal axis of a chart, while the ratio of annual production to cumulative production is plotted on the vertical axis (P=production, Q=cumulative), using the equation $P = a(\frac{1-Q}{Qt})Q$, where a is annual production expressed as a fraction of cumulative production. In early years, production is naturally low, but it is a high percentage of total cumulative production. As time goes on, the cumulative figure goes up, but each year's production is a smaller percentage of the cumulative amount to that date. Thus an entire production history tends to assume a more-or-less straight, downward-trending line.

If production is constrained for part of that time, or, on the other hand, if it is temporarily stimulated, the line will diverge from its previous path. If the method is applied too early in production history, its results will be fairly useless because it takes some time for the linear trend to appear. Also, the technique works best when assessing a large region: in a small area, a single new discovery occurring late in the production cycle can skew the production trend considerably, rendering the earlier trend-line misleading.

Nevertheless, if the region is large and if enough time has passed to enable the data to show a clear trend, it is possible to project that trend-line to the bottom horizontal axis to forecast the ultimately recoverable amount of the resource.

The method has worked well in forecasting ultimately recoverable amounts of oil in many producing nations such as the United States, the United Kingdom, Mexico, and Oman. There is no obvious reason it should fail to apply also to other non-renewable resources such as coal.

David Rutledge, the Tomiyasu Professor of Electrical Engineering and Chair of the Division of Engineering and Applied Sciences at the California Institute of Technology (Caltech), in a presentation at Caltech in October 2007, used the technique to estimate future global coal production, breaking the world up into eight regions — Australia, South

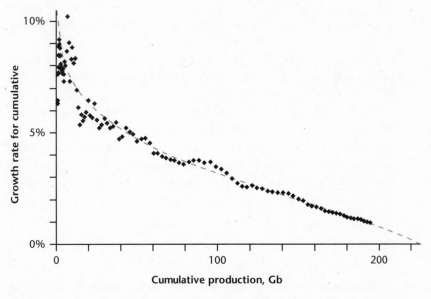

Fig. 5: *Hubbert linearization plot for US oil production from the lower 48 states, showing an ultimate recovery of 225 billion barrels.*

Region	Reserves (Gt)	Trends
North America	255	135
East Asia	190	70
Australia and New Zealand	79	50
Europe	55	21
Africa	30	10
Former Soviet Union	223	18
South Asia	111	
Central and South America	20	
World (at 3.6 boe/ton)	963 (3.5Tboe)	435 (1.6Tboe)
boe = *barrels of oil equivalent* Tboe = *trillion barrels of oil equivalent* [18]		

Asia, East Asia, former Soviet Union, Africa, Europe, South America, and North America — and studying production statistics for each separately. Where no trend became apparent from the application of HL, Rutledge used reserves figures from the World Energy Council (WEC).

Rutledge found about half the reserves officially accepted by the WEC are likely actually to be produced, assuming the HL method holds.

In subsequent communication I've had with Rutledge, he noted that he does not consider HL useful for estimating the timing of the global coal production peak. However, as noted above, the method is used routinely by others for forecasting peaking dates for oil production within individual countries and the world as a whole.

Once about half the reserves are gone, it becomes progressively more difficult to maintain the same or a growing rate of production. The straight-line HL graph can be converted into a logistic curve, with the quantity beneath the curve equal to the ultimately recoverable amount forecast by the first graph. All that is necessary is to take a reciprocal of both sides of the equation:

$$P = a\,\frac{(1-Q)\,Q}{Qt} \qquad \frac{1}{P} = \frac{1}{\dfrac{\{a + (1-Q)\,Q\}}{Qt}}$$

Thus, in principle it is possible to obtain both an ultimately recoverable estimate and a peak production year forecast if there exists a sufficiently robust data set for production over time.

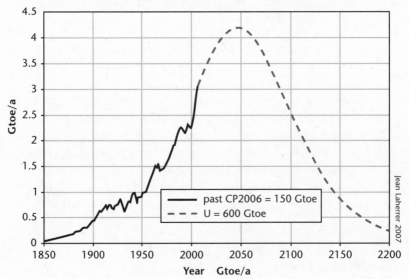

World coal annual production and model for U = 600 Gtoe

Veteran petroleum geologist Jean Laherrère, who served as deputy Fig. 6
exploration manager for TOTAL and has written several reports for
Petroconsultants and *Petroleum Economist* on the world's oil and gas
potential and future production, examined the data for world coal
reserves and production and produced the HL graph of future coal production reproduced here, showing a peak before 2050.[19]

It is worth noting parenthetically that Laherrère prefers to use round
numbers in his calculations. He argues that reserves estimates even to
one decimal place give a false impression of accuracy, where in fact the
numbers are fluid, arguable, and imprecise. This attitude strikes me as
being refreshingly realistic.

5

**"Lignite and Hard Coal: Energy Suppliers for World Needs until
the Year 2100 — An Outlook."** It would be wrong to give the impression that all recent studies have yielded pessimistic results regarding
world coal reserves.

Thomas Thielemann, Sandro Schmidt, and J. Peter Gerling of The
German Federal Institute for Geosciences and Natural Resources (BGR)
have published in the *International Journal of Coal Geology* a report that

forecasts no foreseeable bottleneck in coal supplies and a large potential for coal-to-liquids (CTL). The article's abstract states:

> For three years, international hard coal prices have been at rather expensive levels. Some argue that these higher prices might indicate the threat of a physical scarcity of [coal] — similar to the situation with oil and gas. This is not true. The supply situations with lignite and hard coal appear to be largely not critical. Adjusted to the rise in global coal consumption, which is expected until 2100, nature by and large can meet the world's coal demand. ...The only area of potential concern is Asia (especially China). But today's and coming eager efforts in China to convert coal resources into reserves will most likely deliver the coal needed for the Chinese market.[20]

The conclusion of the report is unequivocal: "Up to the year 2100, and from a geoscientific point of view, there will be no bottleneck in coal supplies on this planet."

The national coal reserves data used in this report are the same set used by the Energy Watch Group.

The BGR authors also assume a slowdown in world demand for coal, from the current six percent annual growth (largely resulting from consumption patterns in China) to two or three percent. They admit that their demand forecast looks "rather conservative," and that stabilization of current high consumption growth is "uncertain."

Fig. 7

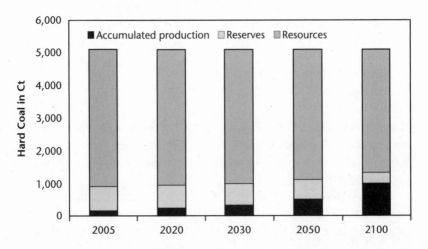

Conclusion

One cannot help but be struck by the dramatic difference in conclusions between the BGR paper on one hand, and the rest of the recent studies and reports on the other. BGR and EWG used the same data; how could they arrive at such divergent outcomes?

Essentially, BGR envisions the large-scale conversion of resources into reserves as a result of increasing investment and the development and deployment of new mining technologies. Most significantly, perhaps, the authors anticipate the conversion of several hundred billion tons of resources into reserves in China, forestalling supply problems there for several decades (EWG foresees significant coal supply problems for China well before mid-century).

The BGR authors do not discuss the historic trend in the opposite direction: in recent decades, and especially in nations with the best reserves-reporting practices, the conversion of reserves to resources has far outweighed the conversion of resources to reserves. Nor do they offer detailed discussion as to why or how this trend will be reversed in the future.

This is essentially the point on which Rutledge has focused his analysis: why have reserves historically been too high, requiring consistent adjustment downward? On the basis of Hubbert linearization analysis, he regards current reserves estimates as representing the *upper limit* of future production, while BGR treats them as the *lower limit*.

The weight of evidence tending toward the more pessimistic conclusions regarding future coal production can only be overcome with detailed data and argument. It is unfortunate in this regard that the BGR paper is relatively brief and does not address many of the questions raised by EWG and Rutledge.

▨ ▨ ▨

We began this chapter with a quote from a booklet titled *The Coal Resource*, published by the World Coal Institute:

> It has been estimated that there are over 984 billion tonnes
> of proven coal reserves worldwide. ...This means that there
> is enough coal to last us over 190 years.

On the basis of what we have seen so far, it seems fair to conclude that the entire statement may be misleading. It is clearly a mistake to use the reserves-to-production ratio in forecasting future supplies. Moreover, the reserves figure, "984 billion tonnes," which sounds solid and authoritative, is in fact arguable.

Coal *resources* certainly exist in great quantities. But resources are of no use if they are inaccessible, are of exceedingly low quality, or are otherwise incapable of meeting the energy needs of modern industrial economies. Therefore we need better answers to the following four questions:

- How much of the resource should currently be counted as reserves?
- How much of the resource might be converted into reserves later as prices rise and new technologies develop?
- What portion of current reserves is likely to be reclassified as resources?
- When will growth in coal production (for the world as a whole, and for significant producing regions) cease and a long decline begin?

Let us keep these questions in mind as we look at resources, reserves, and production in more detail, examining each of the world's primary coal-producing regions.

CHAPTER 2

Coal in the United States

B ECAUSE THE UNITED STATES has the world's largest coal reserves, it has sometimes been called "the Saudi Arabia of coal." It is the world's second-largest coal producer, after China, but surpasses both the number three and four producer nations (India and Australia) by nearly a factor of three.

Wood was this nation's primary fuel until the mid-1880s, when deforestation necessitated greater reliance on abundant coal resources. Coal then remained America's main energy source until the 1930s, when it was overtaken by oil. Today, coal fuels about half of US electricity production and provides about a quarter of the country's total energy.

The United States currently produces over a billion tons of coal per year, with quantities increasing annually. This is well over double the amount produced in 1960. However, due to a decline in the average amount of energy contained in each ton of coal produced (i.e., declining resource quality), the total amount of energy flowing into the US economy from coal is now falling, having peaked in 1998. This decline in energy content per unit of weight (also known as "heating value") amounts to more than 30 percent since 1955. It can partly be explained by the depletion of anthracite reserves and the nation's increasing reliance on subbituminous coal and even lignite, a trend that began in the 1970s. But resource quality is declining even within each coal class.

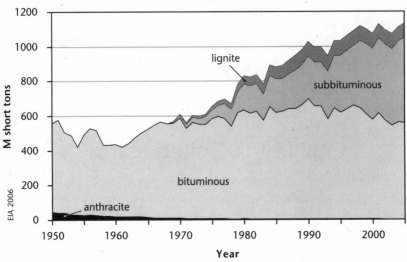

Coal production in USA

EIA 2006

Fig. 8   While there are coal resources in many states, the main concentrations of reserves are in Appalachia, Illinois, Wyoming, and Montana (see
map in Figure 9) The 53 largest coal mines in the United States, located
in just a few states, account for almost 60 percent of total production.

Three states (Pennsylvania, Kentucky, and West Virginia) produce 52
percent of the higher-quality coal in the United States. Coal production
in all three of these states seems to be in decline or at a plateau. Since
the Northeast was the area of the nation earliest settled and was long a
primary center for industrial manufacturing, it is not surprising that the
coal of this region was exploited preferentially. Today, Pennsylvania's
anthracite is almost gone. Mining companies there are now exploiting
seams as thin as 28 inches. West Virginia, the second largest coal-producing state (after Wyoming), where much coal is surface mined by the
environmentally ruinous practice known as mountaintop removal, is
nearing its maximum production rate and will see declines commence
within the next few years, according to a recent USGS report.[1]

The interior region — consisting of Illinois, Arkansas, Indiana, Kansas,
western Kentucky, Louisiana, Mississippi, Missouri, Iowa, Oklahoma, and
Texas — is the smallest coal producer of the three main producing regions.
The Illinois Basin (a region that also encompasses parts of neighboring
states) boasts large reserves of bituminous coal, but production has

US coal deposits

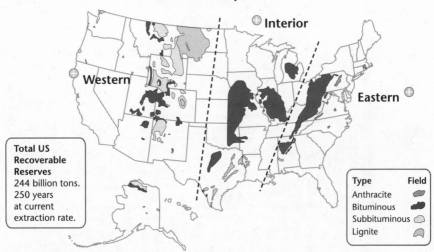

Total US
Recoverable
Reserves
244 billion tons.
250 years
at current
extraction rate.

Type	Field
Anthracite	
Bituminous	
Subbituminous	
Lignite	

fallen there since the mid-1990s. Its coal generally has a high sulfur con-   Fig. 9
tent (three to seven percent), which runs afoul of US environmental
laws, especially the Clean Air Act of 1990. Prior to this legislation,
power plants burning high-sulfur coal released emissions resulting in
acid rain that decimated forests throughout much of the nation. The lignite steam coal of Louisiana is an exception within the region: its sulfur
content is low, so production has risen substantially in recent years. After
2018, sulfur scrubbers will be mandatory for coal-fired power plants in
the United States, perhaps facilitating a move to increase production of
coal from the Illinois Basin.

Wyoming has some bituminous coal, but most of its reserves consist
of subbituminous and lignite. Production from the state (primarily from
the Powder River Basin) has increased sharply since 1970 because its
coal is abundant, cheaply surface-mined, and low in sulfur. Wyoming is
currently responsible for 80 percent of coal production west of the
Mississippi.

Montana also has large deposits of lower-quality coal (subbituminous
and lignite), but these have not been tapped. The current state gover-
nor, Brian Schweitzer, is pushing for development of these resources
using gasification and carbon sequestration technologies, but there are
reasons to doubt whether this will occur soon or on a meaningful scale.

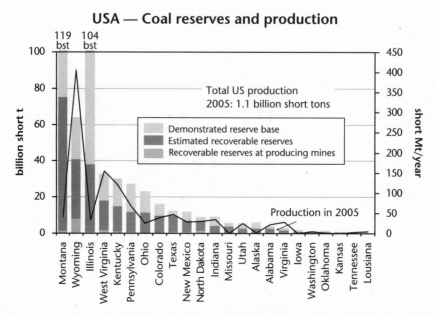

Fig. 10 Montana's coal contains salts that will almost inevitably find their way into the environment if widespread surface mining occurs, contaminating rivers and creating problems for cattle ranching — the state's economic engine and a locus of considerable political clout.

Alaska has extensive coalfields that have yet to be developed due to their remoteness. Promising areas are located in Northwest Arctic, in the region around Healy, in the Mat-Su Valley, and along Cook Inlet. Higher international coal prices could result in the tapping of these resources on a scale that would be economically significant for the state.

For the nation as a whole, future supply hinges on the question of how long rising production of lower-quality coal from Wyoming — supplemented in the future perhaps by coal from Montana and the Illinois Basin — can continue to compensate for declining amounts of high-quality coal from the East. Clearly, the United States has the potential to produce enormous quantities of coal. But the gradual depletion of coal with higher heating value is already necessitating the mining of larger quantities of lower-quality coal to yield an equivalent amount of energy, and, as coal is sourced more from Montana and the Illinois Basin, this will require the building of more rail transport infrastructure and the overcoming of environmental problems and regulatory hurdles.

Over 60 percent of coal mined in the United States is dug from the surface. This is a higher percentage than in most nations, and it is largely due to the contribution of Wyoming. In the eastern states, most coal still comes from deep mines, which are moving toward the recovery of ever-thinner seams. Highwall mining systems and new technologies for longwall mining may lead, ultimately, to remote-control mining involving few or no personnel working underground. These new and more efficient technologies will enable some coal to be mined that would otherwise be left behind, but they are unlikely to be applied throughout the entire industry due to high up-front investment costs.

In surface mining, the largest extraction cost is often incurred in removing overburden (soil and rock). Over the years, the coal industry has introduced ever-larger earth-moving machines for this purpose. However, truck size has probably reached a practical maximum, as the biggest vehicles cannot be maneuvered on roads.

However coal is mined, the industry must always confront the bottom line: the cost of getting coal out of the ground cannot exceed the market price for produced coal. Thus, the current price determines whether marginal coals will be mined profitably, or simply left in the ground. On the other hand, however, as the costs of bringing coal to market rise, this can cause the price of coal to increase — unless and until higher prices suppress demand. If demand for electricity continues to increase (which it has done for decades, up until the current economic crisis), and if cheap alternatives to coal for power generation do not exist in sufficient quantity in the short run, there seems to be no near-term cap to coal prices. As a result, marginal coalfields are now more likely to be mined.

During the two-year period from January 2006 to January 2008, prices rose from about $100 a ton to $250 a ton for high-quality metallurgical grades of US coal. Central Appalachian steam coal rose to about $90 a ton, up from $40 two years previously. During this time production costs rose as well, though not at the same pace.

The cost of producing coal is related to the price of oil. Consider the case of Massey Energy Company, the nation's fourth-largest coal company, which annually produces 40 million tons of coal using about 40 million gallons of diesel fuel — about a gallon per ton (the company also uses lubricants, rubber products, and explosives, all made from petroleum or natural gas). If the price of diesel goes up one dollar, this translates directly to $40 million in increased costs; indirectly related costs also climb.

These costs and prices need to be seen in proportion: while coal generates half of America's electricity, in effect providing much of the essential basis for all economic activity within the country, US coal industry revenues are only about $25 billion — one-tenth those of Wal-Mart.

During some recent years, the United States was a net coal importer, since coal brought by ship from South America was often cheaper to supply to coastal cities than domestic coal brought by rail. This was partly a result of rail transport bottlenecks that are now being addressed with the laying of more rails and the construction of more coal cars. In 2008, however, with coal prices high and imports growing in China and India, the United States began exporting larger quantities. Mines were employing more workers and production was booming. It is still unclear how deeply, and for how long, the current economic crisis will impact America's demand for energy and the price of US coal.

History of Reserves Estimates

The United States has seen a long controversy between coal resource optimists and pessimists — a controversy that is somewhat mirrored in the global coal resource picture.

In 1907, Marius R. Campbell, Director of the USGS, headed the first attempt at a scientific survey of US coal, concluding that ultimately recoverable reserves amounted to 3,157.2 billion tons.[2] Since production in that year was 570 million tons, simple arithmetic yielded an R/P ratio of 5,500/1, which was interpreted as meaning that the nation had a 5,500-year supply. That implied an effectively limitless amount for the practical purposes of economic planning.

Campbell did hedge his estimate by pointing out that much of this coal was not minable, or was inaccessible for other reasons. He also wrote that "... the bulk of coal being mined today is the best in the country, and before long, perhaps before 50 years [i.e., by 1959], much of the high-rank coals will be exhausted." Still, Campbell's figure for total reserves was for many years taken at face value.

Soon, state surveys began gathering more detailed and accurate information, which resulted in the downgrading of regional reserves. Thus, when the US Coal Commission mounted a new survey in 1923, it reduced all state reserves figures and dropped some states entirely from its list of active or likely coal producers. Yet through the early decades of the 20th century, the USGS and the Bureau of Mines stuck to the position that America would have plenty of coal for several millennia.

Shortly after World War II, Andrew B. Crichton, a coal engineer and mine operator in Johnstown, Pennsylvania, undertook a state-by-state informal review of existing reserves estimates, publishing his results in an article titled, "How Much Coal Do We Really Have? The Need for an Up-To-Date Survey," in *Coal Technology* (1948). Crichton minced no words:

> It was asserted at the Denver [USGS] meeting last October that no one should have the temerity to question the Government figures unless they submitted maps and records proving their statements. Well, that is quite a burden to impose upon an individual to justify an opinion regarding our coal reserves. But that is exactly what could be done in many cases in the east where many have knowledge of the wide discrepancy between the Government figures and private records based on prospecting and actual development. It is these wide differences that prompt the fears and lead to the belief that these fantastic and unbelievable figures of the United States Geological Survey are wrong and dangerously misleading and should be corrected promptly.[3]

Citing instance after instance in which USGS reserves figures for well-mined regions had turned out to be highly inflated, Crichton went on to offer his own estimate of national coal reserves as 223 billion tons — a number slightly smaller than today's current official estimate.

Crichton's article, while causing understandable consternation and embarrassment for the USGS, could not be ignored. It was cited repeatedly in Palmer Putnam's authoritative book *Energy In the Future* (1953), which also offered pessimistic assessments of US oil and natural gas supplies.[4] Indeed, Putnam demonstrably erred on the conservative side, forecasting that America's oil production would peak between 1955 and 1960 (the actual peak was in 1970); and that coal production would begin to decline by 1990 — whereas, as we have seen, actual produced amounts continue to grow annually.

The USGS and the Bureau of Mines, which was later absorbed into the Department of Energy, responded by gradually reducing estimates of coal reserves figures for many states and the nation as a whole. Yet through the 1950s, national reserves remained at well over 500 billion tons — still more than 1,000 years in terms of R/P forecasting.

In the 1960s, concerned that reserves figures were not making sufficient allowances for factors that would prevent much of the resource from ever being produced, the USGS commissioned surveys by geologist Paul Averitt, culminating in the publication, in 1975, of *Coal Resources of the United States*.[5] By now the official estimate of recoverable reserves had been whittled down to the current range of 260 to 275 billion tons. This was seen as no cause for alarm, as the reserves-to-production ratio forecast remained comfortably above 200 years; also, it was believed that new technologies (such as longwall mining and underground gasification) would eventually be able to convert substantial quantities of resources back into reserves.

In 1995, the USGS began work on the National Coal Resource Assessment (NCRA), a multi-year effort to create a digital assessment on a region-by-region basis. This assessment is still in process, and few of the crucial results are currently publicly available.[6]

According to the Energy Information Administration's (EIA) website, as of January 1, 2007 the Estimated Recoverable Reserves for the United States amounted to 267 billion tons.[7] Since production for 2006 was 1,162,750 tons, that would indicate an R/P ratio of about 230/1.

A graphic from the EIA, using 2005 data, is helpful in visualizing the various categories within the overall coal resource base (see Fig. 11).

As we are about to see, the long process of revising national coal reserves figures downward may not be at an end.

Recent Studies

1

"**Coal: Research and Development to Support National Energy Policy**" (National Academy of Sciences [NAS], July 2007). This book-length report concluded that "there is no question that sufficient minable coal is available to meet the nation's coal needs through 2030," and also that "there is probably sufficient coal to meet the nation's needs for more than 100 years at current production levels" — though this latter judgment does not appear to be based on a peaking analysis. In sum, however, the report is a plea for better, more realistic reserves estimates:

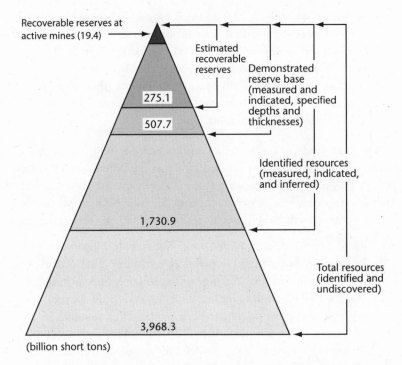

Recoverable reserves at active mines (19.4)

Estimated recoverable reserves

Demonstrated reserve base (measured and indicated, specified depths and thicknesses)

275.1

507.7

Identified resources (measured, indicated, and inferred)

1,730.9

Total resources (identified and undiscovered)

3,968.3

Fig. 11

(billion short tons)

[I]t is not possible to confirm that there is a sufficient supply of coal for the next 250 years, as is often asserted. A combination of increased rates of production with more detailed reserve analyses that take into account location, quality, recoverability, and transportation issues may substantially reduce the estimated number of years' supply. This increasing uncertainty associated with the longer-term projections arises because significant information is incomplete or unreliable. The data that are publicly available for such projections are outdated, fragmentary, or inaccurate.[8]

These doubts about current reserves figures were based upon recent Coal Recoverability Studies undertaken in Kentucky, Illinois, Pennsylvania, and Wyoming — in effect, spot checks to determine whether reserves figures were indeed reliable within restricted areas where coal recoverability could be determined with some accuracy as the result of mining experience.

A total of 65 areas in 22 coal fields have been analyzed, and these studies suggest that 8 to 89 percent of the identified resources in these coal fields are recoverable and 5 to 25 per-,cent of identified resources may be classified as reserves. Because they are based on site-specific criteria, these studies provide considerably improved estimates compared to the ERR [Estimated Recoverable Reserves].[9]

One such study, of the Matewan quadrangle of eastern Kentucky, concluded: "a strong argument can be made that traditional coal producing regions may soon be experiencing resource depletion problems far greater and much sooner than previously thought." [10] The NAS report enumerates the problems that the US coal industry will face in coming decades:

Almost certainly, coals mined in the future will be lower quality because current mining practices result in higher-quality coal being mined first, leaving behind lower-quality material (e.g., with higher ash yield, higher sulfur, and/or higher concentrations of potentially harmful elements). The consequences of relying on poorer-quality coal for the future include (1) higher mining costs (e.g., the need for increased tonnage to generate an equivalent amount of energy, greater abrasion of mining equipment); (2) transportation challenges (e.g., the need to transport increased tonnage for an equivalent amount of energy); (3) beneficiation challenges (e.g., the need to reduce ash yield to acceptable levels, the creation of more waste); (4) pollution control challenges (e.g., capturing higher concentrations of particulates, sulfur, and trace elements; dealing with increased waste disposal); and (5) environmental and health challenges.[11]

2

"Coal: Resources and Future Production (Werner Zittel and Jörg Schindler, Energy Watch Group [EWG], March 2007). This report contains ten pages of analysis specific to US coal supplies.[12] The EWG authors note,

Until the year 2000, productivity [the amount of coal produced per worker hour] steadily increased for all types of coal produced covering surface and subsurface mining. But since then productivity has declined by about 10%. ...The decline in productivity can only be explained by the necessity of rising efforts in production. This might be due to deeper digging and/or to a higher level of waste production. Are these already indications for the era of "easy coal" drawing to a close?

The EWG report offers several peaking scenarios for US coal. The most optimistic shows a peak in 2070.

However, the authors warn that, "Even if volumetric production rates can be increased by about 60% until 2070-2080 before decline sets in, the corresponding energy production will increase only by about 45-50% due to the increased share of subbituminous coal and lignite." Like the National Academy of Sciences, the EWG authors believe that the official estimated recoverable reserves figure is too large. They offer two alternative scenarios for future production: one in which only recoverable reserves at existing mines are considered producible (in which case national production peaks in 2015), and the other in which reported

Fig. 12

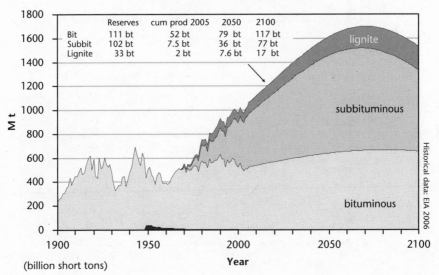

Possible coal production in USA, if 1998 reserves are realistic

	Reserves	cum prod 2005	2050	2100
Bit	111 bt	52 bt	79 bt	117 bt
Subbit	102 bt	7.5 bt	36 bt	77 bt
Lignite	33 bt	2 bt	7.6 bt	17 bt

lignite

subbituminous

bituminous

M t

Historical data: EIA 2006

1900   1950   2000   2050   2100

Year

(billion short tons)

estimated recoverable reserves are all producible, but regional production trends are taken into account (peak occurs in 2040). They suggest that, "The real profile will be somewhere between these two extremes."

A third peaking forecast is based on an LBST ([German renewable energy consultancy] Ludwig- Bölkow-Systemtechnik) analysis, which is

Fig.13

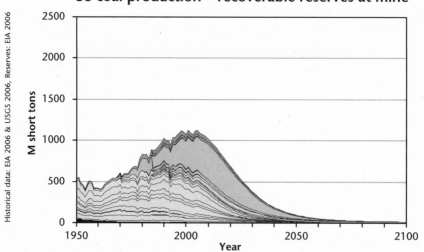

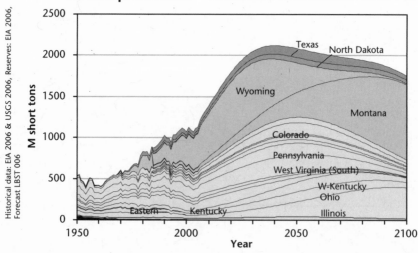

itself based on USGS production forecasts in 2000 using 1995 data.
The USGS forecast is corrected for actual production in the intervening
years, and a future production profile is chosen in accordance with past
production trends and likely production growth (Montana and Illinois
are assumed to provide only marginally increased amounts). It is this
fourth scenario, with a peak around 2025, that the EWG authors appear
to consider most reasonable.

The authors conclude:

> Considering the insights of the regional analysis it is very
> likely that bituminous coal production in the US has already
> peaked, and that total (volumetric) coal production will peak
> between 2020 and 2030. The possible growth to arrive at
> peak measured in energy terms will be lower, only about 20%
> above today's level. ...[T]he 250 billion ton figure [the cur-
> rent official estimate of recoverable reserves] should not be
> the basis for energy planning.

The various EWG scenarios suggest that if Montana and Illinois can
resolve their production blockages, or the nation becomes so desperate
for energy supplies that environmental concerns are simply swept away,   Fig. 14

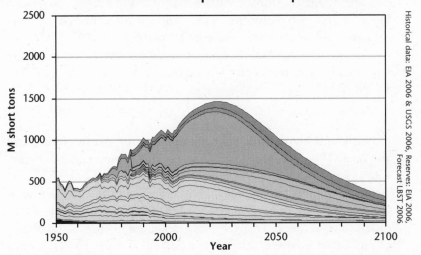

US coal production – LBST forecast with USGS estimate adapted to 2005 production

Historical data: EIA 2006 & USGS 2006, Reserves: EIA 2006, Forecast LBST 2006

then the peak will come somewhat later, while the decline will be longer, slower, and probably far dirtier.

The report contains no discussion of future coal production from Alaska.

3

"The Future of Coal" (B. Kavalov and S.D. Peteves, Institute for Energy, 2007).

Because this report focuses on European energy policy, its discussion of US coal supplies is relatively brief. The authors do note that, "The productivity of [US] coal mines is steadily decreasing," and that, "Their further exploitation is associated with higher costs." Since the main asset of the US coal industry has been its high productivity per miner, "such a development will turn the USA into a high-cost producer no longer competitive on international markets."[13]

The authors also note that:

> The only large potential so far unexploited lies in Alaska. However, these deposits may not come on stream until after 2015. Further delays are possible due to the generally low return on US coal investment, which also affects the upgrading of existing coalfields.

The authors also foresee growing transport problems for US coal: "As with China and Russia, the majority of coal has to be transported inland by rail, which further boosts delivery costs. Railway network capacity is also often insufficient even for current flows."

Their conclusion: "Taken together, the above factors favour cheaper imports, especially from nearby Colombia and Venezuela, thanks to low freight rates."

4

"Lignite and Hard Coal: Energy Suppliers for World Needs until the Year 2100 — An Outlook" (Thomas Thielemann, Sandro Schmidt, and J. Peter Gerling, German Federal Institute for Geosciences and Natural Resources [BGR], 2007). This paper forecasts no bottleneck in coal supplies and a large potential for expanding coal-to-liquids (CTL) production. It offers relatively little detail for individual producing countries and makes no attempt at a peaking analysis. For the United

States, the explicit conclusion is that there will be no coal supply problems this century.[14]

5

"A Supply-Driven Forecast for the Future Global Coal Production" (Höök, Zittel, Schindler, and Aleklett; Uppsala Hydrocarbon Depletion Study Group, 2008). Much of this report repeats data and arguments from the prior EWG publication. The conclusions for the United States are also similar:

> It is reasonable that USA with its huge energy consumption will be among the first in the Big Six to peak in coal production. All major coal-producing states, except Wyoming, seem to be near or past peak production. It should however be noticed that environmental laws and other socioeconomic restrictions probably prevent a significant amount of coal from being produced in the near future, especially high-sulfur coals. A relaxation of the restrictions will therefore probably be able to increase the reserves, but whether this relaxation will happen or not is hard to tell and not considered in the forecast. ...The decline in heat value shows that the best American coals are gone and that poorer and poorer coals are exploited each year. The decrease in mining productivity is also in line with the fact that the most easy-accessible coal is gone.[15]

The authors of "A Supply-Driven Forecast" have produced two peaking charts, one a high-case and the other a low-case scenario. The higher case "depicts a continued rapid expansion of Wyoming together with a build-up of the capacity in Montana." The lower case "does not envision a dramatic increase of the Montanan coal production and consequently the production level from Montana remains at its current level." In the higher case, production peaks around 2040; in the lower case, which the authors regard as "more realistic," the decline commences around 2030.

6

Hubbert linearization and curve-fitting. David Rutledge argues that, in any region for which we have something close to a complete production history (e.g., British coal), historic reserves estimates typically have

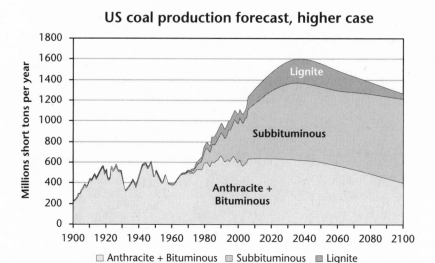

US coal production forecast, higher case

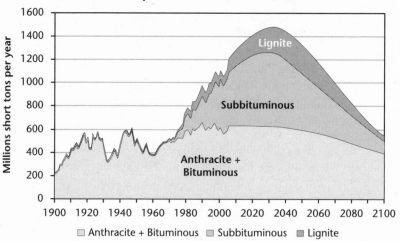

US coal production forecast, lower case

Fig. 15   turned out to be too high.[16] As we have seen, this position is now in effect supported by NAS on the basis of recent site-specific case studies. Rutledge goes on to argue that Hubbert linearization often yields a more accurate forecast of ultimately recoverable reserves.

Rutledge applies linearization to North American coal producing regions, "with trends for the East (40 Gt), West (25 Gt), reserves for

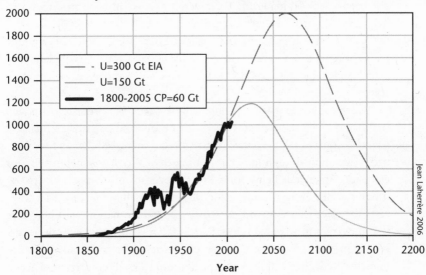

US coal production with models for U=300 Gt & 150 Gt

Legend:
- U=300 Gt EIA
- U=150 Gt
- 1800-2005 CP=60 Gt

Year

Jean Laherrère 2006

Montana (68 Gt), and trends for Canada and Mexico (2 Gt total)." This results in an estimate of total ultimately recoverable reserves of 135 billion tons, roughly half the reserves figure now used by official agencies.

Veteran petroleum geologist Jean Laherrère has charted two Hubbert curves for US coal,[17] one assuming an ultimate production of 150 billion tons (which is roughly in line with Rutledge's conclusion just cited), and the other assuming 300 billion tons (which is somewhat more than the current official ERR). The production peak in the former case occurs in 2025; in the latter case, decline commences after 2060.

Fig. 16

Implications

With oil and natural gas prices becoming alarmingly volatile, the return of the United States to a greater reliance on coal might seem inevitable. The nation paid nearly $600 billion for petroleum imports in 2008, and this ongoing transfer of wealth abroad cannot help but have a substantial negative impact on the domestic economy. There are three ways to moderate that impact: reduce consumption of liquid fuels through conservation; produce more fuels domestically; or electrify transport, which will require more electricity. Coal could help with either of the latter two strategies. Given that the nation possesses so much coal, and that energy from coal is still relatively cheap, it would seem inevitable that strong arguments will be made for a dramatic increase in coal production to help solve the nation's energy problems.

Yet if most of the recent analyses cited here are correct, this strategy has a short shelf life. Within the planning horizon for any coal plant proposed today lie much higher coal prices and perhaps even resource scarcity.

The sheer amounts of coal that will be needed in order to offset any significant proportion of current or future oil (and perhaps also natural gas) consumption, and to meet the projected increased demand for electricity, are mind-boggling. Coal is a lower-quality fossil fuel in the best case, and America is being forced to use ever lower-quality coal. Just to offset the declining heating value of US coal while meeting EIA forecasts for electricity demand growth by 2030, the nation will then have to mine roughly 80 percent more coal than it is currently mining. If carbon sequestration and other new technologies for consuming coal are implemented, they will increase the amount of coal required in order to produce the same amount of energy for society's use, since the energy penalty for capture and sequestration is estimated at up to 40 percent. A broad-scale effort to produce synthetic liquid fuels from coal (CTL) will also dramatically increase coal demand. If the current trend to expand coal exports continues, this would stimulate demand even further. Altogether, there is a realistic potential for more than a doubling, perhaps even a tripling, of US coal demand and production by 2030 — which would hasten exhaustion of the resource from many current mining regions and draw the inevitable production peak closer in time.

Assuming this higher demand scenario (from CTL, increased exports, and growing electricity consumption), by 2030 the nation's dependence on coal will be much greater than is currently the case, and coal's proportional contribution to the total US energy supply will have grown substantially. But at the same time, prices for coal are likely to have increased precipitously because of transport bottlenecks and higher transport costs (due to soaring diesel prices), falling production trends in many current producing regions, and the lack of suitable new coalfields. The interactions of high and rising coal prices with efforts to maximize output are hard to predict.

As limits to domestic coal production appear, exports could diminish and there could instead be efforts to import more coal, probably from

South America. But in that case the US economy would suffer increasingly from economic dependencies and geopolitical vulnerabilities that already hobble the nation as a result of its oil imports.

It may be tempting to think of coal as a transitional energy source for the next few decades, while a longer-term energy strategy emerges. But in that case, an important question arises: Will there be sufficient investment capital and technical resources in three or four decades to fund the transition to the *next* energy source, whatever it may be? By that time (assuming EIA projections are reasonably accurate), demand for energy will be higher. The price of oil, gas, and coal will be higher — perhaps much higher — and so the nation will be spending proportionally much more of its GDP on energy than it does now. Meanwhile, the energy cost of building new infrastructure of any kind will be higher. Therefore, it is likely that insufficient investment capital will be available for the large number of new energy projects required. The transition if deferred will thus be more expensive and difficult than it would be now. Indeed, the longer a transition to an ultimate (and sustainable) energy regime is put off, the harder that transition becomes.

Coal currently looks like a solution to many of America's fast-growing energy problems. However, this is a solution that, if applied on a broad scale, seems certain only to exacerbate the nation's energy dilemma in the long run, as well as contribute to an impending global climate catastrophe.

United States: Category	Amount (billion short tons)
Recoverable Reserves at Active Mines	19
Estimated Recoverable Reserves	270
Demonstrated Reserve Base	490
Identified Resources (from Averitt, 1975)	1,700
Total Resources (above plus undiscovered resources)	**4,000**

CHAPTER 3

Coal in China

Overview

CHINA IS THE WORLD'S FOREMOST COAL PRODUCER AND CONSUMER, surpassing the United States by a factor of two on both scores and accounting for 40 percent of total world production. Moreover, its coal consumption has been rising rapidly, at a rate of up to ten percent per year (which translates to a doubling of demand every seven years). While China is a significant producer of oil and natural gas, coal dominates the nation's fossil-fuel reserve base. About 70 percent of China's total energy is derived from coal, and about 80 percent of its electricity. The country has recently become the world's foremost greenhouse gas emitter due to its growing, coal-fed energy appetite.

This nation's coal-mining history is probably the world's longest, dating back two millennia — though modern mining methods were not introduced until the late 19th century by European, and later by Japanese, companies. Production achieved one million tons per year in 1903, growing at an average annual rate of over ten percent. Growth slowed during the civil wars of the 1920s, but resumed strongly in the mid-1930s. After the establishment of the People's Republic in 1949, coal production again slumped, then quickly increased to over 400 million tons per year by 1960, only to fall again during the turbulent years of the Cultural Revolution. Production accelerated from the 1970s on, achieving one billion tons per year by 1989. In 1996, China began addressing problems of mine safety and low productivity by closing its smallest and least efficient mines. This led to a temporary decline in production lasting until 2000; since then, production has grown with astonishing rapidity to the present annual output of roughly 2.5 billion metric tons (tonnes) or 2.7 billion US short tons (2,000 pounds).

China's coal consumption in 2000 was 30 times its volume a half-century earlier, at the time of the establishment of the People's Republic. And just since 2000, consumption has more than doubled.

China currently has roughly 25,000 coal mines, with 3.4 million registered employees. Many of these mines are small, private, local — and even illegal — operations that can respond quickly to the market; but they are less efficient than larger, centralized mines and tend to have more environmental and safety problems.

The productivity of China's coal mining is low: in 1999, 289 tons of coal were produced per miner averaged across all the nation's mines, versus almost 12,000 tons per miner in the United States. This productivity rate resulted from still-low levels of mechanization within the mining industry. However, the strong trend during the past decade has been toward greater mechanization.

Thin overburden allows surface mining in some areas, but only four to seven percent of China's reserves are suitable for surface mining, and of these, most consist of lignite. Today the average mining depth in China is 400 meters, a figure that is slowly increasing, and 95 percent of mines are shaft mines[1] (compared to 48 percent in the United States). Uncontrolled underground coal fires, some of which will burn for decades, have become an enormous environmental problem in China, consuming an estimated 200 million tons of coal annually — an amount equal to about 10 percent of the nation's coal production. These ultra-hot fires can occur naturally, but most are caused by sparks from cutting and welding, electrical work, explosives, or cigarette smoking. Across the northern region of Xinjiang, fires at small illegal mines have resulted from miners using abandoned mines for shelter, and burning coal within the shafts for heat. China's underground coal fires make an enormous, hidden contribution to global warming, annually releasing 360 million tons of carbon dioxide — as much as all the cars and light trucks in the United States.

The pace of China's headlong dash toward increased coal consumption is legendary: in recent years an average of one new coal-fed power plant has fired up every week. The resulting annual capacity addition is comparable to the size of Britain's entire power grid. The price being paid in environmental quality and human health for this coal bonanza is likewise well known — to citizens and visitors alike: coal power plants emit deadly clouds of soot, sulfur dioxide, and other toxic pollutants, as well as millions of tons of carbon dioxide. As a consequence, areas in southern China such as Sichuan, Guangxi, Hunan, Jiangxi, and Guangdong have increasing problems with acid rain; many of China's cities are shrouded in a continual pall of smoke reminiscent of London or Pittsburgh in 1900; and respiratory ailments now account for 26 percent of all deaths.

China's coal is used not only for electricity generation, but also for the production of iron, steel, and building materials (primarily cement), and as fertilizer feedstock. These main drivers of increased demand are themselves powered by heavy industrial growth, infrastructure development, urbanization (roughly 300 million additional people will live in Chinese cities by 2020), and rising per-capita GDP.

All of these trends in turn emerge from China's recent history. At the end of the Communist revolution in 1949, the country was impoverished and war-ravaged; the overwhelming majority of its people consisted of rural peasants. Communist Party chairman Mao Zedong's stated goal was to bring prosperity to his populous, resource-rich nation. A period of economic growth and infrastructure development ensued, lasting until the mid-1960s. At this point, Mao appears to have had second thoughts: concerned that further industrialization would create or deepen class divisions, he unleashed the Cultural Revolution, lasting from 1966 to the mid-1970s, during which industrial and agricultural output fell. As Mao's health declined, a vicious power struggle ensued, from which emerged the reforms of Deng Xiaoping. Economic growth became a higher priority than ever before, and it followed in spectacular fashion from widespread privatization and the application of market principles. "To get rich is glorious," Communist officials now proclaimed.

During the 1950s, '60s, and '70s, the populace worked hard, sacrificed, and endured grinding poverty for the good of the nation. Now a small segment of that populace — mostly in the coastal cities — is enjoying a middle-class existence, and in some cases spectacular riches. This wealth disparity is sustainable only as long as the middle class continues to expand in numbers, offering the promise of economic opportunity to hundreds of millions of poor peasants in the interior of the country if they migrate to the cities.

In effect, rapid economic expansion and increasing prosperity (for a small, influential portion of the population) are being used to divert domestic attention from frustrated democratic political aspirations and regional rivalries. But China's central government has unleashed a firestorm of entrepreneurial, profit-driven economic activity which it cannot effectively contain. China's central government and its legal institutions are relatively weak; meanwhile the uncontrollably dynamic economy is export-dependent and ill-suited to meeting domestic needs.

In short, China has encouraged rapid export-led economic growth as a way of putting off dealing with its internal political and social problems. Economic growth requires energy, and China's energy comes overwhelmingly from coal. The nation's short-term survival strategy thus centers on producing enormous quantities of coal today, and far more in the future.

However, there are signs that China's domestic coal production growth may not be able to keep up with rising demand for much longer.

As in the United States, coal transport bottlenecks raise production costs and inhibit growth. Coal transport by rail has grown faster than road and water transport. But only half of China's coal production is from rail-connected mines. Lack of rail capacity is leading to increased demand for diesel fuel for coal trucks, and thus to higher diesel prices (and increasingly frequent shortages), and these in turn result in more coal delivery problems.

The lack of diesel fuel for coal transport could potentially be solved by turning coal into a liquid fuel (a process discussed in more detail in Chapter 7). China's largest coal firm, the Shenhua Group, recently opened the country's first coal-to-liquids (CTL) plant, and announced plans to start seven more by 2020. Other CTL plants were also planned — including several in Northern China that Shenhua would construct with partners Shell and Sasol, slated to open in 2012; and one planned by the Yankuang coal group, the second-largest coal producer in China, near Erdos. However, many of these new CTL plants have since been canceled due to projected high costs.

If only a few of these proposed CTL plants are constructed, China will lead the world in production of synthetic liquid fuels from coal. But even if all of them were to come on line, this would offset only a small portion of China's oil imports (the recent goal was to produce 286,000 barrels per day by 2020, while the nation currently imports over three million barrels of petroleum per day, with that amount growing rapidly). In any case, CTL will entail substantial new coal demand as well as severe environmental consequences. According to China's Coal Research Institute, each barrel of synthetic oil produced from coal will consume at least 360 gallons of fresh water. For comparison: 360 gallons equals roughly 8.5 barrels; thus at this ratio of CTL to water, 286,000 barrels per day (bpd) of CTL would require approximately 2.5 million bpd of water, or 100 million gallons per day. And most areas of China are already experiencing water scarcity.

The irony inherent in China's grand experiment with CTL is that in order to solve coal supply problems stemming from diesel shortages, the country must produce even more coal.

Aside from transport bottlenecks, supply problems are also resulting from ongoing crackdowns on mines that are unsafe, polluting, or wasteful of energy.

China is producing its best coal first. The country has yet to exploit its reserves of lignite, which has high moisture and ash content and entails much higher CO_2 emissions. A new technology (Integrated Drying Gasification Combined Cycle, or IDGCC) developed in Australia and now being studied by the Chinese government, is capable of burning this coal efficiently and reducing greenhouse gas emissions; but if lignite grows as a share of total coal production, this will exacerbate transport problems, because much more material will have to be mined and moved in order to deliver the same amount of energy.

All of these difficulties with producing and delivering sufficient coal are leading to increased imports. China has been an international coal supplier since the early 20th century, when nearly all its exports went to Japan. In 2001, China's coal exports amounted to 90 million tons. But Chinese coal imports doubled between 2005 and 2007, making the nation a net importer of the resource. This trend toward increasing coal imports, which is driving up international coal prices and impacting the economies of other coal importers such as India and Japan, seems almost certain to accelerate.

China's electric power generation is becoming more efficient, but even an extensive rollout of the highest-efficiency plants could only dent growth in coal consumption before 2020. Meanwhile, these new power plants will impose greater up-front costs, driving up the price of electrical power in the country.

In sum, continually increasing coal consumption is central to China's economic existence; however, there are signs that the country is already experiencing difficulty in maintaining its furious growth pace in producing the resource. The amount of coal available in the future will crucially determine the direction of the nation's economy and likely its internal social and political stability as well.

Resource Characteristics and History of Reserves Estimates

China's coal resources are concentrated mainly in the northern half of the country, with fully half of all reserves located within the three provinces of Inner Mongolia, Shanxi, and Shaanxi. Reserves comprise the complete range of coals, from lignite to anthracite, with bituminous the most abundant (according to the 1992 WEC reserves estimate, which is borrowed by BP for its annual statistical review, 13.5 percent of China's coal reserves consist of lignite, 24 percent non-coking bituminous coal, 28 percent coking bituminous coal, and 18.5 percent anthracite[2]). Locally, seam quality is highly variable, although sulfur levels are in most cases low.

Fig. 17   While recoverable reserves are a matter for debate, China's total coal resources are clearly vast, with government figures listing a resource base

China's major coal fields and mines

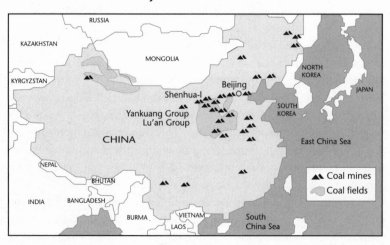

of about a trillion tons. As is the case elsewhere, location, seam thickness, quality, and depth determine how much of the resource will ever be mined. China's coal reserves to a depth of 150 meters are relatively small, with resources at depths of 300-600 meters forming the majority of the future reserve base.

Early reserves estimates of China's coal were imprecise because thorough surveys were impeded by the turbulence of the nation's political history during the last century. In the 1930s, reserves were estimated at somewhat over 200 billion tons, sufficient for over 5,000 years of production at then-current levels of output.[3]

In 1987, the BP "Statistical Review of World Energy" listed reserves of 156.4 billion tons. In 1990, BP reported Chinese coal reserves as 152.8 billion tons. By 1992, the amount had fallen to 114.5 billion tons.[4] Oddly, that official number has not changed in the succeeding 16 years, during which time the nation has produced over 20 billion tons of coal.

There are differing opinions on this anomaly: the World Energy Council politely notes that it "indicates a degree of continuity in the official assessments of China's coal reserves." However, Energy Watch Group calls that reasoning "strange," since Chinese coal reserves had been downgraded two times since 1987, evidently at least partly due to the subtraction of produced quantities.

Reserves were thrown further into question in 2002, when the Chinese Ministry of Land and Natural Resources declared that the country's proven recoverable coal reserves amounted to 186.6 billion tons. However, this large number has not been adopted by the World Energy Council, the International Energy Agency, or the BP "Statistical Review."

Recent Studies

1

"Coal: Resources and Future Production" (Werner Zittel and Jörg Schindler, Energy Watch Group [EWG], March 2007).

As noted above, the EWG authors question the WEC figures for China's reserves, pointing out that these evidently do not account for amounts produced since 1992, nor for amounts lost to coal fires (EWG does not discuss the much larger reserves number published by the Chinese government). The report's authors write:

China's reported coal reserves are 62.2 billion tons of bituminous coal, 33.7 billion tons of subbituminous coal and 18.6 billion tons of lignite. Subtracting the produced quantities since 1992 (the latest data update) results in remaining reserves of about 44 billion tons of bituminous coal, 33.7 billion tons of subbituminous coal and 17.8 billion tons of lignite.[5]

This indicates total remaining recoverable reserves of about 96 billion tons. EWG uses this updated reserves figure (which still does not account for amounts lost to uncontrolled underground coal fires) to plot a possible future production profile, using a logistic curve. Their results:

This scenario demonstrates that the high growth rates of the last years must decrease over the next few years and that China will reach maximum production within the next 5-15 years, probably around 2015. The already produced [cumulative] quantities of about 35 billion tons will rise to 113 billion tons (+ 11 billion tons of lignite) [by about] 2050 and finally end at about 120 billion tons (+ 19 billion tons of lignite) around 2100. The steep rise in production of the past years must be followed by a steep decline after 2020.

The EWG authors restate their conclusion several times: "either the reported coal reserves are highly unreliable and much larger in reality than reported, or the Chinese coal production will reach its peak very soon and start to decline rapidly."

In addition to near-term peaking in quantities of coal produced, declining coal quality is also a problem: "projected produced quantities of coal will show a steadily declining energy content." Currently, China produces very little of its lignite. This is likely to change as higher-quality coals are exhausted. But the nation's lignite reserves are too small to have much influence on total coal production, and lignite's energy content is only about one-quarter that of high-quality bituminous coal.

The EWG report discusses China's plans for CTL development, suggesting that this will hike coal demand by "several hundred million tons per year," pushing the nation's production capacity "very fast to its limits."

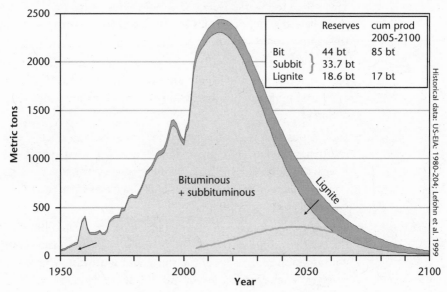

Coal production in China

Historical data: US-EIA: 1980-204; Lefohn et al. 1999

2

"The Future of Coal" (B. Kavalov and S.D. Peteves, Institute for Energy, 2007).

Fig. 18

This report implies considerable skepticism about China's future coal supplies. After noting that the great bulk of the nation's reserves are at some depth, the authors state that, "Developing new underground mines takes 4-5 years on average. This means that no major incremental growth in reserves can be expected by 2010."[6] In a series of summary bullet points, they further point out that,

- Any intensive development of new coalfields will put equipment suppliers and markets under enormous pressure. For strategic reasons, China has always preferred national coal mining technologies to foreign technologies. It is rather uncertain whether even domestic and foreign manufacturers of mining equipment together will be able to meet such a huge increase in demand. Even if they manage to do so, it would anyway be achieved at much higher prices, which will subsequently be reflected in coal production costs.

- Productivity and recovery rates in Chinese mines are much lower than the world averages. Other things being equal, this means that deposits twice as large are needed to extract the same amount of coal.

- For decades, China has had the worst coal mine safety records in the world. With the increase in living standards, poor coal mine safety is becoming a growing issue in the country.

- Indigenous coal is of acceptable, but not very high quality. It has a relatively high sulphur and ash content that lowers the calorific value. Coal washing is one way of overcoming this problem, but it is difficult, increases costs and causes large energy losses.

- The vast majority of coal deposits in China are located in the north and north-east of the country, while the main consumption centres are in the south and southeast. This involves long-distance, expensive transport by railway, which significantly pushes up the final delivery cost. For the southern coastal regions, therefore, it is more cost-effective to go for imports from Indonesia, South Africa or Australia than for indigenous coal from the north.

3

"What Is the Limit of Chinese Coal Supplies — A STELLA model of Hubbert Peak" (Zaipu Tao and Mingyu Li, *Energy Policy*, 2007).

These two authors, from the Northeastern University PRC School of Business and Administration, apply Hubbert analysis (linearization and peaking) to Chinese coal production, basing their analysis on the official Chinese government proven recoverable reserves figure of 186.6 billion tons. In doing so, they use STELLA, a software platform for modeling the behavior of complex, dynamic systems.

Tao and Li write that Hubbert linearization indicates yet-to-produce reserves of 71.73 billion tons, with a maximum production rate of 1.41 billion tons/year; the all-time production peak occurred in 2006. But this cannot be correct, as in fact the current production rate is much higher and production continues to increase. The problem, the authors suggest, is that linearization in this instance gives a false result for yet-to-produce

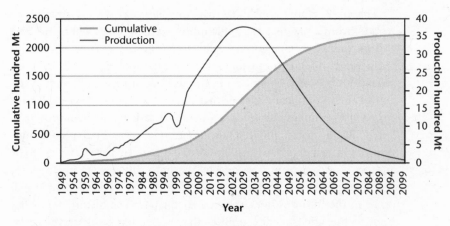

Fig. 19: *The standard run (K = 2226 hundred billion tons).*

reserves: "We know," they write, "that the number should be the official government figure of 186.6 billion tons." Therefore they substitute that amount in the equations, with the result that, "According to the standard run, the Hubbert Peak for China's raw coal production appears to be in 2029 with a value of 37.84 hundred million [i.e., 3.7 billion] tonnes."[7]

The STELLA software allows for the addition of various parameters (such as annual reserves additions, growth rates, and CO_2 emissions), and results in differing decline curves. Tao and Li conclude:

> According to this simulation ... the peak in China comes between 2025 and 2032 with peak production about 3339-4452 million tons. Chinese raw coal output will grow by about 3-4% annually before the peak, which probably is a good chance for the development of China's coal industry. However, the corresponding amount of greenhouse gases produced may act as an enormous obstacle to increasing the coal production. ...To meet the increasing demand, China should consider new energy development policies related to supply diversification before the peak comes.

4
"Lignite and Hard Coal: Energy Suppliers for World Needs until the Year 2100 — An Outlook" (Thomas Thielemann, Sandro Schmidt, and J. Peter Gerling, German Federal Institute for Geosciences and Natural Resources [BGR], 2007).

The BGR report concludes that for China, as for the rest of the world, "from a raw-material angle in this scenario there will be no bottleneck in coal supplies until 2100."[8] However, the assumptions and reasoning that lead to this judgment are questionable in light of considerations brought up by EWG. The BGR authors write: "Should the annual rise in output be greater than 1%/a [per annum], Asia will have to convert resources into reserves on a much larger scale than presumed here." But as noted above, China's rate of growth in coal consumption has in fact recently been closer to 10 percent per year. The BGR authors do not explain how or why that rate will slow so much. Also, the conversion of resources to reserves that the authors assume will occur in the future is not explained adequately. The historic trend has been in the opposite direction — that is, for booked reserves to be downgraded to mere resources — and it is unclear why that trend should reverse itself.

The BGR authors do note that, "Since it will certainly be possible to cover some needs on the world market, the pressure of Asia, specifically China and India, on world coal supplies and world market prices will be much higher than today."

5

"A Supply-Driven Forecast for the Future Global Coal Production" (Höök, Zittel, Schindler, and Aleklett; Uppsala Hydrocarbon Depletion Study Group).

As in its other country analyses, this paper's discussion of China's future coal production expands on the reasoning and conclusions of the EWG report. It concludes:

> The forecast estimates that Chinese coal production will reach a peak in 2020, perhaps even earlier if the reserves are backdated to 1992, when the last actual update took place, and corrected for cumulative production. So China might be very close to its maximum coal production unless the reserves are larger than reported or a significant amount of resources can be transformed into produced volumes in the near future. Unless something dramatic happens to the Chinese reserves the future production will very soon end up under reserve constraints.[9]

The authors of this paper have produced two new charts, one based on reported reserves, the other based on reported reserves minus amounts produced since 1992:

Fig. 20

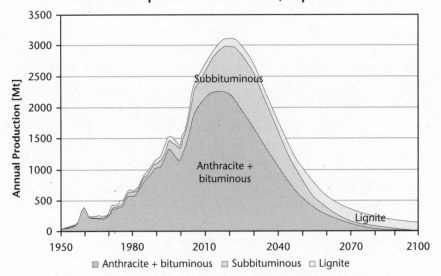

China coal production forecast, reported reserves

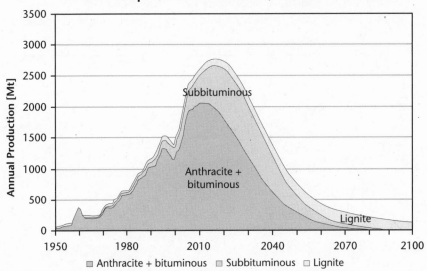

China coal production forecast, backdated reserves

6

Other Hubbert linearization and curve fitting (David Rutledge and Jean Laherrère).

In applying the Hubbert linearization method, David Rutledge of Caltech finds the trend line for China's total ultimate production to be 115 billion tons, with 45 billion tons produced so far and 70 remaining.[10] This agrees well with the result obtained by Tao and Li. Like them, he questions this result. He notes that while the trend line that now shows 70 billion tons left to produce has been steady for 40 years,

> ...in the last three years, production has gone through the roof. There may be a move to a new trend line underway. It is also possible that production will come back to the original trend line. During the Great Leap Forward from 1958 to 1960, reported production soared for a few years, but returned afterwards to previous rates.

Veteran petroleum geologist Jean Laherrère has charted a Hubbert curve for future Chinese coal production, assuming an ultimate production of 150 billion tons,[11] a figure similar to those used by the Energy Information Administration of the US Department of Energy and the BGR. This assumes 110 billion tons of remaining reserves, an amount somewhat higher than EWG but slightly lower than the WEC number, and much smaller than the official Chinese government's 186.6 billion tons. Nevertheless, in this model, production peaks at

Fig. 21

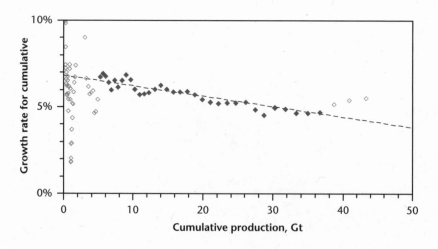

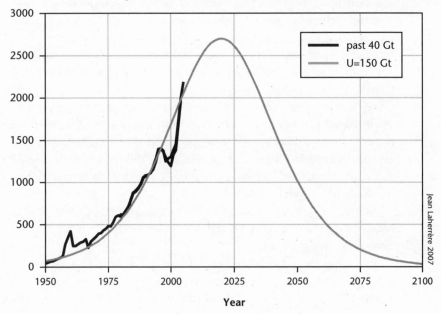

China coal production with ultimate 150 Gt (EIA, BGR)

Jean Laherrère 2007

about the same time as suggested by EWG and Höök et al. — that is, in 2020.

Fig. 22

Implications

Demand for coal in China is growing so quickly that even if the high reserves estimate from the Chinese government of 186.6 billion tons proves to be accurate (as opposed to EWG's much lower estimate of 96 billion tons), this may shift the date of peak production by only about 5 to 17 years — from the years 2015-2020 (EWG) to 2025-2032 (Tao and Li). This further calls into question the BGR conclusion that "there will be no bottleneck in [China's] coal supplies until 2100," as a delay of the peak to that extent — by more than 65 years beyond the Tao and Li forecast range — would require a conversion of resources to reserves on a truly monumental scale. Such a conversion is impossible to justify by precedent, and so BGR's conclusion can only be considered realistic if China's coal demand is assumed to level off soon and perhaps fall in the coming decades — in which case a production peak will have occurred in effect.

But such demand reduction is currently difficult to envision. China's economy has been, is, and will continue to be coal-powered — as long as sufficient supplies are available — since few options exist to substantially reduce its coal dependency. Offsetting one year of recent coal demand growth would require over 100 billion cubic meters (bcm) of new natural gas production capacity (current total capacity is 76 bcm), 85 GW (gigawatts) of hydropower capacity (current total capacity: 83 GW), or nearly 50 GW of nuclear power (expected total capacity by 2020: 40 GW). It must be emphasized that these offsetting amounts are required *yearly* additions. Even if the amount needed to offset coal growth were spread among these and other alternatives such as wind and solar, the required additions would be economically daunting if not physically impossible to achieve.

As a result, China's practical ability to make serious CO_2 emissions reductions in the years ahead is very low, unless energy demand and production decline sharply.

It is important to note that the current global economic crisis does indeed seem to be resulting in slowing Chinese energy demand, though at this writing the degree of demand reduction likely in the next few years is impossible to assess.

China's demand for coal will grow even faster than it has recently if CTL technologies are implemented at the scale and speed now proposed. Coal-to-chemicals plants, now being considered, would have a smaller impact, but in the same direction. Coal-to-liquids and coal-to-chemicals are projected to add 450 million tons of annual new coal demand by 2025. In this case, total demand could exceed 4.7 billion tons by 2020.

The studies cited here (with the exception of BGR) suggest that China's domestic coal production growth cannot be sustained much beyond 2020; indeed, in the most constrained case (that is, if the EWG forecast is correct), demand will outstrip domestic supply dramatically during the next ten years.

China's demand for coal imports will therefore almost certainly top 200 million tons per year by 2020, and could exceed that figure by a wide margin. This will significantly impact regional markets, leading to increased competition with other coal-importing countries (Japan, South Korea, Taiwan, India, and Europe), and to much higher prices for internationally-traded coal. (Currently, the total annual volume of internationally-traded coal is just over 800 million tons.)

The supply problems discussed here appear already to be manifesting. During the winter of 2007-2008, power plants in many parts of the country ran short of coal due to soaring prices and transport bottlenecks, while snow and ice storms disrupted power transmission. A *People's Daily* article, quoting Zhang Guobao, deputy head of the National Development and Reform Commission, noted that only a "fragile balance" existed in the thermal coal market despite huge and growing coal output.[12] During that same winter, prices for internationally-traded coal climbed substantially.

Fig. 23

China coal
From 2006 to 2007 : Imports increased by 120%

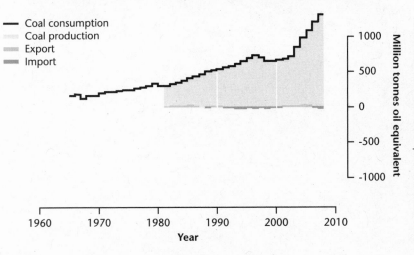

Coal consumption
Coal production
Export
Import

Million tonnes oil equivalent

1000

500

0

-500

-1000

Year

1960   1970   1980   1990   2000   2010

Data: BP Statistical Review 2008 Graphic: mazamascience.com

China's furious pace of economic growth, which is often touted as a sign of success, may turn out to be a fatal liability. Simply put, the nation appears to have no Plan B. No fossil fuel other than coal will be able to provide sufficient energy to sustain recent economic growth rates in the years ahead, and non-fossil sources will require unprecedented and perhaps unachievable levels of investment just to make up for *declines* in coal production — never mind providing enough to fuel continued annual energy *growth* of seven to ten percent per year.

If and when China ceases to have enough new energy to support continued economic growth, there are likely to be unpleasant consequences for the nation's stability. If such consequences are to be averted, the country's leadership must find ways to rein in economic growth while reducing internal social and political tensions, meanwhile investing enormous sums in non-fossil energy sources. A serious attempt to reduce greenhouse gas emissions would entail an identical prescription. It is a tall order by any standard, but serious contemplation of the alternative — which, in the worst instance, could amount to social, economic, and environmental collapse — should be bracing enough to motivate heroic efforts.

CHAPTER 4

Coal in Russia and India

Russia

Overview

ACCORDING TO THE WORLD ENERGY COUNCIL, the Russian Federation has the highest coal reserves-to-production ratio for any nation in the world, at 500:1. This should not be taken to mean that the country has 500 years worth of coal, for reasons discussed at length in Chapter 1; nevertheless, the figure is not without significance. Russia's official coal reserves are the world's second-largest, and many of its potential coalfields have yet to be developed.

Coal dominated Russia's energy history from the late 19th century until the 1960s, when the country's vast reserves of gas and oil began to be vigorously exploited and major coal-producing areas in the Donetsk Basin neared exhaustion. Coal-powered industry was the backbone of early Soviet industrial expansion, and many industrial centers were sited near coal mines.

Coal production reached 121 thousand tons annually in 1860, grew quickly to 12 million tons (Mt) in 1900, and then to 34.5 Mt in 1916.[1] During and shortly after the 1917 revolution, production sharply declined and most mines were destroyed. In the 1920s, dozens of mines were restored and new ones developed, including some opencast mines. In the decade from 1928 to 1938, more than 200 mines were constructed, adding another 100 Mt of capacity.

Germany's occupation of the eastern regions of the USSR during World War II resulted in the loss of 60 percent of previous coal production. This was compensated for by the intensive development of new production in areas further west that permitted surface mining (by 1945, opencast mines were producing 17.8 Mt, or almost 12 percent of total coal production).

The Soviet Union's introduction of a new holiday — "Miners Day" — in 1947 demonstrated the prestige with which the profession was then regarded.

Mining science advanced during the 1960s and '70s and large-scale manufacturing of modern mining equipment began. In 1988, coal production in Russia reached a peak of 425.4 Mt, but then gradually declined due to the age of the majority of mines, as well as their increasing average depth. Mine safety was becoming a more serious issue, contributing to mass strikes by miners in 1989-1990. Coal miners, who had been among the best-paid industrial workers of the Soviet era, were now experiencing long delays in receiving wages, as the nation's economy nosedived.

In the early post-Soviet era, drastic measures were required to avert a collapse of the coal industry. These included the closing of the most dangerous mines and the privatization of others. Production in 1998 was 231 Mt — down by almost half from the peak in 1988. Still, during this time 11 new underground and 15 opencast mines were constructed in Kuzbass and other regions with a total capacity of 57 million tons per year. As a result of mechanization, the cost of coal production declined and productivity increased; employment in the coal sector fell from 900,000 in 1991 to 400,000 in 2001.[2] In the near future, the trend for improvement in productivity is likely to continue as Russia's coal industry adopts more state-of-the-art machinery and practices.

While Russia's coal industry was entirely state-owned during the Soviet era, private companies now account for more than 60 percent of domestic production and about 80 percent of exports.

Currently, hard coal production still takes place in the Russian part of the Donetsk Basin, near Ukraine, as well as the Kuznetsk and Pechora basins south of the Urals. The coal reserves in eastern Siberia and the Russian Far East, which consist mostly of subbituminous coal and lignite, are largely unexploited because of lack of transport infrastructure and distance from markets.

Russia's total coal production in 2007 was 347 million tons, growing at a rate of just over two percent per year, while domestic consumption was about 261 million tons.[3]

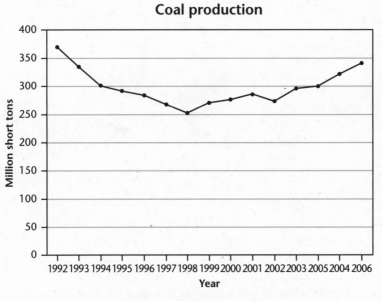

Coal production

Fig. 24a

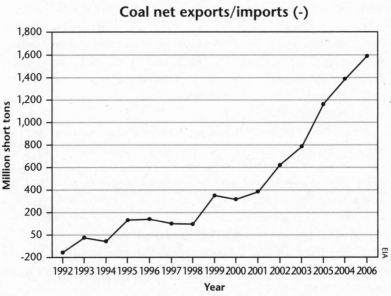

Coal net exports/imports (-)

Fig. 24b

Fig. 25   Coal provides around 17 percent of Russia's primary energy and 30 percent of its electricity production. These percentages are expected to increase as Russia raises the share of its coal used internally so as to be able to export a greater proportion of its natural gas, which is easier to transport and more lucrative to sell internationally.

About 20 percent of Russia's coal production is exported, more than half of that to Europe, and exports have been increasing dramatically in recent years. Indeed, most of the recent industry growth has been due to heightened exports. However, the Russian coal export industry suffers from high costs for transportation and port fees, and this may inhibit future export growth.[4]

Meanwhile, Russia's domestic demand for coal is increasing as many new coal-fired power stations are being built (an additional 40 to 50 GW of capacity is expected to be installed between now and 2020, by which time domestic coal demand is expected to double).[5] In 2008, Russia faced the possibility of a hydropower shortage, which created more short-term domestic demand for coal. But even without the hydropower shortage, Russian coal exports were expected to decline by 10 to 12 million tons the following year.[6] This new trend for declining coal exports will likely continue, and Russia could well cease being an exporter within only a few years.

History of Reserves Estimates

During the Soviet era, recoverable coal reserves were estimated to be in the range of 300 to 400 billion tons — equivalent to about 30 percent of current total world reserves. However, the Soviet regime evaluated mineral resources using economic criteria different from those employed in the West. After the collapse and break-up of the USSR, new reserves definitions and estimation practices were introduced, taking into account minimum seam thickness, ash content, unfavorable geological conditions, and the remoteness of many coalfields. The resulting re-estimation of reserves is still ongoing, and will undoubtedly remove a substantial portion of current reserves from the national inventory when completed. The 2007 edition of the BP "Statistical Review" and the WEC both list Russia's total coal reserves as 157,010 million tons. When better reporting practices are fully adopted this figure could decline by up to a third.[7]

Recent Studies

1

"Coal: Resources and Future Production" (Werner Zittel and Jörg Schindler, Energy Watch Group [EWG], March 2007).

The EWG Report does not include a separate annex on Russia. The authors' expectation, as represented in their graph for future world coal production (see Figure 4 in Chapter 1), is for an increase in production from this country lasting until about 2050, with only a very slow decline afterward. However, they note that "it is by no means certain that [the] reported reserves [of former Soviet Union countries, principally Russia] will ever translate into corresponding production volumes."[8] They justify this by noting that:

> Some doubts regarding the data quality of the coal reserve data for the former Soviet Union countries remain as the last update was carried out in 1998. Therefore, it is probably more realistic to expect the decline after peak to be steeper than shown in the [world future coal supply] figure.

2

"The Future of Coal" (B. Kavalov and S.D. Peteves, Institute for Energy, 2007).

This report offers a pessimistic assessment for prospects of Russian coal. After discussing the problems with the eastern coal reserves' location and lack of rail and seaport facilities, the authors note that, "Consequently, Russia is a relatively expensive producer of coal, competitive on the world market only when international coal prices are high."[9] They point out also that Kazakhstan is in a similar situation.

To make matters worse, "Coal production and exports suffer from a generally low level of mechanization and productivity, as well as poor mine safety."

The report's conclusion is that, "Taking into account all the above factors, Russia no longer appears to be a coal-rich country."

3

"Lignite and Hard Coal: Energy Suppliers for World Needs until the Year 2100 — An Outlook" (Thomas Thielemann, Sandro Schmidt, and J. Peter Gerling, German Federal Institute for Geosciences and Natural Resources [BGR], 2007).

This report offers few specifics regarding future trends for Russian coal. However, due to higher consumption rates in the United States, the authors conclude that, in the period from 2050 to 2100, Russia will retain the "biggest hard coal reserves, with an abundant 129 Gt (40% [of world total]) in 2100, followed by North America (94.9 Gt, 29.6%), Oceania (34 Gt, 10.6%), [and] Asia (31.6 Gt, 9.8%)."[10] The passage would seem to indicate that the authors expect Russia's reserves to grow dramatically during the century, although the recent trend has been toward downward revision.

4

"A Supply-Driven Forecast for the Future Global Coal Production" (Höök, Zittel, Schindler, and Aleklett; Uppsala Hydrocarbon Depletion Study Group).

This paper, unlike the earlier EWG report, does offer a section specifically devoted to Russia's future coal supplies. Its conclusions are somewhat self-contradictory, however. While the section begins with the broad and reassuring statement that, "Russian coal reserves are vast, and will be more than enough for the future with expected production and demand trends," it goes on to say that, "In reality this would mean a large-scale development of the Siberian reserves."[11] However, the authors note the difficulty of this actually occurring:

Russia has plenty of new coal regions that can be developed, but most of these are located in Siberia or the eastern parts of Russia. Much of the coal is thus essentially stranded inside Siberia, far from potential markets and major consumption regions. An improvement of the transportation systems is needed to make these coal regions really useable. The Russian coal assets in Siberia are comparable with the situation in Montana. Due to the remoteness from the market and the huge need for infrastructure investments in new coalmines, transport systems, and trade ports it is very questionable if they ever will be developed.

Höök et al. note that "[Russian] coalfields near Europe are declining and will have to be abandoned sometime in the future," and that, "The majority of the Russian coal deposits [i.e., those in Siberia] are subbituminous and lignite, thus making them less suitable for longer transport and export." The section ends with an upbeat but somewhat perplexing statement: "The production forecast does not consider any of the problems mentioned here as constraints and depicts a continued production growth as new areas and mines are brought into production as long as the reserves allow."

5

Hubbert linearization.
David Rutledge finds that the Hubbert linearization trend for Russia's coal production indicates remaining reserves of only 30 billion tons.[12] This apparently very low figure results from the fact that Siberian resources are for the most part yet to be tapped, and therefore do not contribute to the trend. Thus, the figure should be regarded as the lower boundary on future production, in the case that transport issues or other problems prevent the far-eastern deposits from being developed.

Implications

Russia is one of the few nations that may be able to count on coal as a primary source of energy for several decades to come — even with slowly growing rates of consumption; but this outcome hinges almost entirely on the development of Siberian reserves. There are mines already operating in the region, where mine safety is an issue. However, expansion

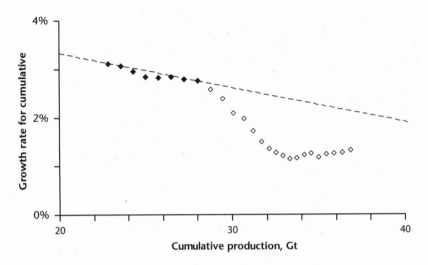

Fig. 26   of mining activity in Tunguska and regions further east will require overcoming not only safety problems, but daunting logistical hurdles as well,
especially with regard to transportation.

There are currently approximately 20,000 rail wagons in Russia, but
old wagons are falling apart three times as fast as they are being replaced.
About 10,000 new wagons — which cost $40,000 apiece — are needed,
but they are in short supply even when there is investment capital available to purchase them.[13]

Because much of the eastern coal is of low quality, long-distance
transport either to population centers in the east or to seaports in the
west may be hard to justify on economic grounds. A solution could be
to build power plants close to mines and transmit electricity to western
markets — but this would also entail huge infrastructure investments.

Further, expansion of mining in Siberia will entail horrific environmental costs. Surface mining would result in deforestation or would
disrupt environmentally sensitive tundra; meanwhile, indigenous peoples throughout the sparsely populated region — which is already
hard-hit by the effects of climate change — would be displaced or would
suffer further degradation of their fragile ecosystems.

All of these considerations play into the question of Russia's actual
coal reserves. If it is assumed that Siberian coal will be developed on a
grand scale, then the nation's reserves are correspondingly large. If Siberia
is assumed to continue being a minor coal producer, then Russia's coal

reserves may already be largely tapped out: accepting the Hubbert linearization trend identified by Rutledge (which includes very little contribution from Siberia and sees 30 billion tons remaining) as a likely limit on future production, this would suggest that Russia's peak in coal production will occur very soon or may already have passed.

Russia certainly has incentives to develop its eastern coal resources: while the nation's oil and gas are still plentiful, these can be exported to earn foreign exchange income; coal is more sensibly used domestically. Russia's oil production has been falling recently, and many analysts believe that the decline will continue.[14] Nevertheless, the country is still vying with Saudi Arabia as the world's largest oil producer. Russia's Gazprom, which sells natural gas to Europe, has recently become the world's largest energy company. Higher-grade fossil fuels are supplying Russia with both cash and geopolitical clout. Therefore the nation's leaders would no doubt prefer to maximize these benefits by running the domestic economy more intensively on coal.

Thus, efforts surely will be made to develop Siberia's coal, though it is unclear how far those efforts will proceed before practical limits constrain them. Meanwhile, the looming consequences for the expansive eastern region will likely provoke a political backlash from indigenous rights groups.

Because Siberia's coal is of relatively low quality, it will produce high carbon emissions relative to energy; thus the development of this resource would also prevent Russia from honoring existing or future climate accords.

One path would avert many of these problems: Russia could build highly efficient gasification power plants in Siberia, sequester carbon, transmit electricity to markets in the west and to China, and contribute financially to the economic welfare of the indigenous peoples of the region. This would be an extremely expensive strategy to pursue. Moreover, at some point, it would become a problem not merely of financial return on financial investment, but of energy return on energy investment: if energy profit ratios drop much below about ten to one, the effort to provide energy to society itself begins to take up a disproportionate share of society's energy budget. Only a complex and extensive study will determine how much of Siberia's coal can potentially be extracted and used while delivering substantial net energy, but the Russian government would be well advised to undertake such a study before committing itself to the large-scale development of its eastern coal deposits.

India

Overview

India's situation is somewhat similar to that of China, in that it is a populous country experiencing fast economic growth based largely on coal. Consumption of the resource increased from 360 million tons in 2000 to 460 million tons in 2005 — a growth rate of 5.5 percent per year. Coal now provides 53 percent of India's total energy. It is the nation's most abundant fossil fuel, and 68 percent of India's CO_2 emissions are from the burning of coal. The country's coal R/P ratio exceeds 200, well above the world average.[15]

Coal production commenced early in this nation's colonial history, when Warren Hastings began commercial mining in West Bengal in 1774. However, lack of transport facilities resulted in minimal development until 1900, when rail infrastructure began to knit the region together. Production capacity reached six million tons per year by the early 1900s. Following independence in 1947, output accelerated; and the pace grew once again following the formation of the nationalized company, Coal India, in the early 1970s. By the end of the 1990s, India ranked third in world hard coal production, behind China and the United States.

Nearly all of the nation's coal is produced by the state-owned monopoly, Coal India Ltd. (CIL), which is the world's largest coal company, with 473 mines and 424,000 employees.[16] Coal India expects its production to achieve 520 million tons by 2011-12 and 665 million tons by 2016-17.[17]

India's coal is distributed over a number of relatively small basins, mostly in the eastern and southeastern regions. Nearly all the deposits are of hard coal, with some lignite in the northwestern region which is mined for electricity generation; however, most of the resource is of low grade and of low quality, with unusually high ash content. This makes Indian coal unsuitable for export, and it also creates unusually high amounts of fly ash at the country's power stations.[18]

More than three-quarters of India's coal is produced by surface mining; underground mining accounts for the remaining output, and most of the latter is accomplished by room-and-pillar methods.

Aside from resource quality, the main problem for India's coal industry continues to be lack of sufficient transportation infrastructure. A little over half of mined coal is hauled by rail, almost 20 percent by truck, and the rest by sea and other means (including conveyor belts and ropeways). Truck transport is becoming increasingly expensive as a result of high diesel fuel prices, and rail infrastructure is inadequate to move growing quantities of coal.

India's coal consumption is now slightly under 500 million tons per year, while production is running at just over 400 million tons.[19] The shortfall of about 100 million tons needs to be made up by a growing share of imports. However, the number of Indian ports that can handle coal is limited, and a lack of rail wagons and a shortage of locomotives makes it difficult to reliably transport coal from port to power plant even when imports are available.

Fig. 27

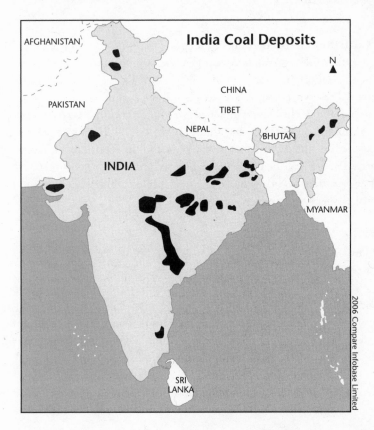

Recently the nation's power plants faced coal shortages, as CIL lowered its supply projection for 2008-09 from 305 million tons to 292.15 million tons.[20] This is a clear indication that the infrastructure constraints described above are already having a serious impact on India's coal industry.

History of Reserves Estimates

Indian hard coal reserves were upgraded from 12.6 billion tons in 1987 to 90 billion tons in 2005. This is the only instance globally of such a large and recent expansion of reserves (Australia has also posted reserves increases, but on a smaller scale). However, in the WEC 2007 survey, India reduced its reserves from 92Gt to 56Gt, which reflects a transition in reporting from "coal in place" to "recoverable coal."

Recent Studies

1

"Coal: Resources and Future Production" (Werner Zittel and Jörg Schindler, Energy Watch Group [EWG], March 2007).

This report has very few details on India's coal. The large, recent upward reserves revisions are noted, and the authors point out that, "All other countries have individually downgraded their hard coal reserves by a combined 35 percent over the same period."[21] Their general conclusion is that "the data quality is very poor and the reported data cannot be regarded as a realistic assessment of 'proved recoverable coal reserves'";[22] however, they do not provide any evidence or argument regarding data quality specific to India.

2

"The Future of Coal" (B. Kavalov and S.D. Peteves, Institute for Energy, 2007).

This report points out the problems of resource quality noted above and goes on to say that, "Although the gross R/P ratio is high, the amount of realistically exploitable reserves is uncertain."[23] The authors offer a fairly detailed assessment of India's daunting challenges with developing its coal industry further:

- At present, most Indian coal is mined at depths of 150-300 metres. The deposits at such depths may be sufficient

for 50-60 years only. The recovery of deeper reserves may
be precluded by excessively high costs.

- Most coal mines are state-owned, a fact that constrains private investment in the sector. Investment in coal supply is
particularly impeded by distribution regulations and control over foreign investment.
- The operation of coal mines is outdated and productivity
is very low compared to international standards, especially
in underground mining.
- Most coal deposits are located in the northeast part of the
country, while the major consumption centers are in the
west and southwest (including coastal) areas of the country. Bringing coal to the major consumers, especially in
unwashed form, involves expensive transport by rail over
large distances (500-750 km). Transport costs may account
for up to 70% of total delivery costs.
- For a number of reasons, including the presence of three
different gauges, the condition of the Indian railways is far
from perfect. Improving the railways calls for huge investment, which does not seem realistic in the foreseeable future.
- For these reasons, and also to improve average coal quality, many power plant operators in the west and southwest
parts of India are importing increasing volumes of higher-
quality steam coal.
- The power generation sector is heavily regulated and electricity prices are kept at very low levels that basically
preclude investment. Power plant operators have little
incentive to invest in improving coal quality, the development of logistical infrastructure or the modernisation of
power plants.
- Most power plants are over-aged, outdated, and consequently inefficient.

3

**"Lignite and Hard Coal: Energy Suppliers for World Needs until
the Year 2100 — An Outlook"** (Thomas Thielemann, Sandro Schmidt,

and J. Peter Gerling, German Federal Institute for Geosciences and Natural Resources [BGR], 2007).

This report provides no detail on India. The most relevant passage may be: "Asia's ... thirst for energy will pose huge challenges for Asia's energy supply throughout the entire century, from a deposit standpoint it will be possible to cover the rising demand using Asian coal deposits and the world market."[24]

4

"A Supply-Driven Forecast for the Future Global Coal Production" (Höök, Zittel, Schindler, and Aleklett; Uppsala Hydrocarbon Depletion Study Group).

The authors note that, "Tata Power, India's largest power company in the public sector, signed a contract with an Indonesian coal company, which entitles Tata Power the right to buy 10 Mt of coal annually."[25] This raises the question: "If the Indian coal supply was reliable and vast, why sign such an import contract?" They go on:

> Also Tata Steel, another giant company of Tata Group, entered a memorandum of understanding with Riversdale Mining and acquired a 35% stake of its Mozambique coal projects and earlier signed an agreement with an Australian company for a 5% share of a coal project in Queensland. These can also be seen as signs that the Indian coal reserve is actually smaller than reported or that a large part of them is unusable for commercial enterprises or possibly that imported coal is cheaper.

Nevertheless, Höök, et al., use the stated reserves figure in their forecast for future global coal supply: "The production forecast does not take any of the mentioned economic problems into account and only portrays a logistically increasing production in line with the reserves."

5

Hubbert linearization.

David Rutledge writes that, "For South Asia, and Central and South America, there has been exponential growth in recent years, so there is no trend."[26] Therefore, for the purposes of assessing global recoverable reserves, he simply adopts the published reserves figures — which, he notes, "are likely to be too high."

Implications

India will likely remain a highly coal-dependent nation for many years to come, since it has few other options for generating increasing amounts of electricity. Electricity demand is set to expand along with the nation's fast-growing economy. Currently the electrification rate is still low, especially in rural areas, where the average grid connection level is only 30 percent.

But, as with China, limits to domestic coal supplies may loom sooner rather than later. As Kavalov and Peteves point out, transportation is a limiting factor; but also, for India, there are serious problems with resource quality, which may call current reserves figures into question. Further, because so much of India's coal is surface mined, a substantial expansion of production in this very populous nation will likely entail not only deforestation and other environmental consequences, but also the removal of many villages. Such a massive relocation of people would pose daunting social and political challenges for the affected regions, and possibly for the central government as well.

The solution — already being implemented — is simply to import more coal. But imports are likely to be impeded by poor port infrastructure and resulting port congestion and vessel delays (on top of the usual heavy delays during the monsoon season). And the lack of adequate rail infrastructure connecting ports with power plants must also be addressed.

Further, since other nations in the region are also looking to buy more coal on the international market, prices for imported coal are likely to rise considerably in the years ahead. Given the size of India's economy, even a modest increase in imports will challenge the capacity limits of international suppliers.

Altogether, then, India's coal dependency poses extremely serious economic, social, and environmental problems for the nation's future. As international coal prices rise, the nation is likely to endure economic contraction, unless alternative sources of energy can be developed extremely rapidly.

As of July 2008, India's energy shortages appeared even more serious than those in China. Its nuclear power plants are failing for lack of water, as is hydropower — both because glaciers in the Himalayas are melting due to global warming. Over 85 percent of India's oil is imported and domestic prices are subsidized. The resulting increased fuel costs are taking a heavy toll on the state budget. While the situation in India is not yet as bad as that in neighboring Pakistan, blackouts and liquid fuel shortages are being reported almost daily somewhere in the country. There is no end in sight to this situation other than through falling energy demand resulting from the global financial crisis.

CHAPTER 5

Coal in Australia, South Africa, Europe, South America, Indonesia, and Canada

Australia

Overview

A USTRALIA IS THE WORLD'S LEADING COAL EXPORTER by a wide margin; in 2006 it exported 233 million tons out of its total production of 309 Mt.[1] The nation accounts for 29 percent of all world coal exports. Its people have the highest per-capita rate of greenhouse gas emissions (10.1 tons annually), due to high energy consumption and high coal consumption relative to other energy sources.

Of Australia's coal exports, 80 percent are bound for Asia. Over half of Australia's coal is exported to Japan; next in line are Korea and Taiwan — though the share going to China and India is expected to grow substantially in coming years. A small fraction (12 percent) currently goes to Europe, while the remainder is shipped mostly to South America.[2] The export of coal accounted for almost 20 percent of total Australian commodity income in 2006. In 2005-2006 the nation's income from international coal sales increased by 43 percent compared to 2004-2005.[3]

Nearly 80 percent of Australia's electricity comes from coal-fired power plants, and about 40 percent of its total energy. Coal production has more than doubled in the past 25 years, and has grown 36 percent over the last decade alone.

Coal was first discovered in Australia in 1791 by a convict, William Bryant, at the mouth of the Hunter River in New South Wales (NSW). The first coal mining settlement was established there in 1801.[4] Coal was found on the Brisbane River and near Ipswich in the mid-1820s when the new settlement of Brisbane was in its infancy, and the first coal mine opened in Queensland in 1843. Smaller coal deposits were also discovered in other states.

In early colonial years, coal was used mostly for home heating and cooking. By the second half of the 19th century, railroads and steamships were using the bulk of Australia's coal. By 1888, annual coal production in NSW and Queensland had topped 2.5 million tons.

At the beginning of the 20th century, coal was also used to produce gas to light and heat cities and towns. During and after World War II, demand for coal-fired electricity generation grew quickly, and in the 1950s and '60s coking coal began to be exported to Japan for the burgeoning steel industry there. International sales of steam coal started in the late 1970s.

Australia's coal deposits are plentiful and of high quality. They are suitable for surface mining, which ensures high recovery rates, high productivity per miner, and low production costs.

Most Australian coal deposits are located in the eastern part of the nation, with smaller coal-bearing areas in Western Australia and central Tasmania. Together, Queensland and NSW account for almost 97 percent of Australia's annual coal production and all of the nation's black coal exports. Thick, flat-lying seams are common. Many of the coal regions have coal with low ash and low sulfur content, while some even have good coking properties, making them useful for steel production.

The Tertiary basin in Victoria contains lignite seams that reach an enormous thickness of 230 meters.[5] This coal is used exclusively for local power generation.

Nine coal terminals at seven ports handle the coal exports. The total capacity is approximately 237 Mt, but different expansions are needed and are being planned.

Most of the producing mines are located relatively close to the coast, and when they are depleted, new mines need to be opened further away, thus calling for more transport. This will lead to higher coal costs.

History of Reserves Estimates

Australia has managed to increase its reserves by a moderate amount over the last two decades. As of 2004, Australia contained 86.5 billion short tons (Bst) of recoverable coal reserves, the majority of which are concentrated along the country's eastern seaboard.

Recent Studies

1

"Coal: Resources and Future Production" (Werner Zittel and Jörg Schindler, Energy Watch Group [EWG], March 2007).

This report contains relatively little detail concerning Australia, other than to note the upgrades of Australian hard coal reserves in recent years.[6]

2

"The Future of Coal" (B. Kavalov and S.D. Peteves, Institute for Energy, 2007).

Kavalov and Peteves offer a good overview of Australia's coal prospects, noting that, while "The recent sharp increase in world coal demand and hence trade has cut the Australian R/P coal ratio by almost 40% — from 297 years at the end of 2000 to 213 years at the end of 2005," nevertheless, even if these trends continue, "proven reserves should still be sufficient by 2020."[7] According to the authors, the following are the main challenges on the horizon for Australia's coal producers:

> [T]he cost of developing new coalfields will certainly be higher, as the new deposits tend to be located further away from the major exporting facilities. Of more concern is the need to expand export facilities, mainly the seaport infrastructure. The recent troubles and delays in vessel handling in the major Australian coal exporting terminals have strengthened these fears.

Still, on balance, the report foresees "bright prospects for the Australian coal industry and exports."

3

"Lignite and Hard Coal: Energy Suppliers for World Needs until the Year 2100 — An Outlook" (Thomas Thielemann, Sandro Schmidt, and J. Peter Gerling, German Federal Institute for Geosciences and Natural Resources [BGR], 2007).

The BGR authors note that Australia's "very large reserves" will be considerably depleted by 2100, but no actual supply shortfalls are envisioned.[8] The report is written with European energy import requirements in mind, and therefore notes that "due to high transport costs" it makes little sense for Australia to sell its coal to Europe on a large scale. "Nevertheless, exchanges of traded quantities between the two markets did increase in the last two years, accounting for about 7% of the traded hard coals in 2005."

4

"A Supply-Driven Forecast for the Future Global Coal Production" (Höök, Zittel, Schindler, and Aleklett; Uppsala Hydrocarbon Depletion Study Group).

Like Kavalov and Peteves, these authors see few near-term problems for the Australian coal industry other than transport issues:

> Australia can expand its production but the bottleneck is the transportation systems that allow coal to be sent for export. Expensive new infrastructure is needed for a major expansion. In the future the coal producing regions will move towards central Australia, thus distancing the mines from the export terminals and the domestic consumption centres.[9]

In their global forecast, Höök et al. do not take into account potential impacts from transport bottlenecks on future Australian coal exports.

5

Hubbert linearization.
David Rutledge finds a trend for 50 Gt remaining, with 79 Gt official reserves.[10] This should be regarded as a lower limit.

Implications

Australia clearly has abundant coal for domestic consumption for many decades to come. However, it is the future of the nation's export capacity that will have enormous implications not only for its domestic economy, but for those of other key nations as well. Australia's coal exports are of increasing importance for growing markets in China and India, as well as existing customers in Japan, South Korea, and Taiwan.

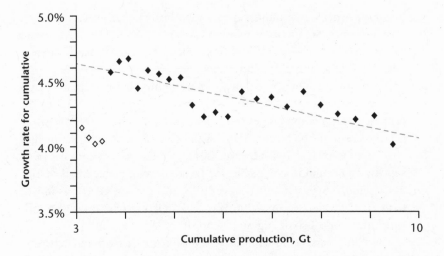

Fig. 28

Continuing to increase the scale of Australia's total coal production and export capacity will pose a growing challenge. New mines will be located ever further away from coal ports, and the increased costs for land transport (exacerbated by skyrocketing diesel prices) will inevitably raise coal prices for offshore delivery. Australia will need to build new rail infrastructure to accommodate these increasingly lengthy overland shipments — at the same time it will be needing new rail and light rail passenger lines to facilitate travel and commerce in the wake of quickly rising prices for gasoline, diesel, and jet fuel. Therefore, competition for limited capital available for transport infrastructure development could pose a political as well as an economic problem in coming years.

The combination of growing competition for Australia's coal (from China and India) and domestic transport limits could force up the price of internationally-traded coal very quickly — and to unprecedented levels — within only a few years.

South Africa
Overview
Any discussion of Africa's coal must inevitably focus almost exclusively on one nation — South Africa — since nearly all of the continent's reserves and current production are located there. The nation is currently a significant exporter, with 80 percent of exports going to Europe.[11] And it is the world's leader in the use of coal-to-liquids (CTL) technology.

South Africa's coal industry has a long history that goes back more than a century. Significant expansion came after World War II, and coal exports began in the late 1970s. Since then, the country has become a reliable supplier of high-quality steam coal.

Most of the country's coal deposits are located in its north and eastern areas, in a series of basins with varying characteristics. About 60 percent of production comes from underground mines, with this share set to increase in the future. Many of the thickest seams of high-quality coal have been depleted; however, some prime coal blocks have been kept by large mining companies for future development. South Africa has around 5.5 percent of the world's coal reserves, all consisting of hard coal. Production in 2006 was 244 million tons, making South Africa the world's sixth largest coal producer.[12]

Over the years, South Africa's coal production has been matched by the development of new deposits. Consequently, the country's R/P ratio is still above 200.

Much of the expansion in domestic production since 1973 resulted from South Africa's response to an apartheid-era oil embargo. Coal-to-liquids technology had previously been used by Germany during World War II; South Africa's Sasol Corporation refined the process and built a complex at Secunda that still produces about 150,000 barrels of synthetic diesel fuel per day, providing about 30 percent of the nation's liquid fuel.[13] However, this single plant uses a significant share of South Africa's coal production (45 million tons per year), and also produces a disproportionate amount of greenhouse gas emissions and other pollution.

South Africa exports about 30 percent of its annual coal production, which accounts for around 55 percent of the industry's profits. This large dependence on exports (exceeded only by Australia) makes South Africa's coal industry especially sensitive to fluctuations in international coal prices.

Export capacity is limited partly by harbor infrastructure, and the country is addressing this problem with a project in Richards Bay Coal Terminal with an aim to expand capacity from 73 million tons to 91 Mt per year.[14]

Much of the nation's future coal production will be in the Waterberg region, near Botswana, where half of remaining reserves are located. All major coal companies are now prospecting there or applying for prospecting rights. However, many improvements in infrastructure (especially transportation) are needed if this area is to become a large coal producer.

History of Reserves Estimates

South Africa is one of the few countries with reserves continuously shrinking by quantities roughly in line with annual production. Current reserves stand at 48.75 billion tons (as of the end of 2006).[15]

Recent Studies

Neither the EWG report ("Coal Resources and Future Production") nor the BGR report ("Lignite and Hard Coal: Energy Suppliers for World Needs until the Year 2100 — An Outlook") contains any discussion specific to South Africa.

1

"The Future of Coal" (B. Kavalov and S.D. Peteves, Institute for Energy, 2007).

This report discusses South Africa's current and future coal production in some detail, since it is written from a European perspective and the country is a major supplier of coal to Europe. Its conclusion is that "increasing and even maintaining production and export volumes in the future may pose challenges for several reasons," which include the following, quoted from the report:[16]

- Most currently operated mines are approaching the end of their economic life. There is a common consensus that the development of new reserves will be much more costly than the development of the old deposits.

- In addition, the quality of the coal from these new reserves is considered to be less than the quality of coal from existing fields.

- Taken together, these factors may result in proven reserves lower than the current estimates.

- The majority of the new deposits tend to be located further away from the main export terminals. This implies the need to develop completely new logistics chains and costly infrastructure. The capacity of the railway network, operated by the state-owned company Spoornet, is of particular concern. Securing sufficient port handling capacity, along with the related investment funds, is another important challenge for South African coal exports.

- The wide spread of AIDS/HIV amongst mineworkers presents another very serious risk for the coal industry in South Africa.

2

"A Supply-Driven Forecast for the Future Global Coal Production"
(Höök, Zittel, Schindler, and Aleklett; Uppsala Hydrocarbon Depletion Study Group).

This paper contains a fairly detailed country assessment of South Africa, which includes the following conclusions:[17]

- The majority of the remaining reserves are thus low-grade coals, difficult to mine, located in small blocks or such. It is still possible to mine coal for at least 40 to 50 years more, with current and new technology, but the low-cost mega-mines are something of the past.

- Since South Africa deals with an increasing amount of low grade, high ash coals, coal-washing processes have become important to improve the coal and make it more suitable for international trade. This leads to large "stockpiles" of discarded waste coals. Currently these stockpiles exceed the 1 billion [ton] mark. In 2003 the volume of waste coal, resulting from the washing processes, reached 63 million tons, almost as large as the export volume the same year.

- The South African coal production is becoming increasingly dependent on smaller fields and lower quality coals, which leads to higher production costs. The days of easy coal are nearing an end.

- South Africa has the potential to increase its export to some extent. The environmental problem caused by the large piles of waste coal might be problematic in the future, as there already are public complaints about the increased number of smaller coal mines and the transportation of coal by truck.

• Also the rising domestic demand for coal may cause impact on the export. There is a huge need of more electricity and new coal-fired plants are built to match the increasing demand.

The report's forecast for future global coal supply does not include these mentioned problems as constraints.

3

Hubbert linearization.
David Rutledge finds a trend for 10 billion tons of reserves-yet-to-produce — only a little more than one-fifth of the reserves officially stated.[18] This should be accepted as a lower limit to future production, as new regions near Botswana have yet to be tapped and do not contribute to the trend.

Implications

Over the past year South Africa has become mired in an electrical power crisis, with Eskom, the nation's state-run energy company, struggling to keep the lights on as power demand has outstripped supply. Part of the problem is that it has been 20 years since the newest power plant was built; meanwhile, many of the nation's poorer citizens who previously

Fig. 29

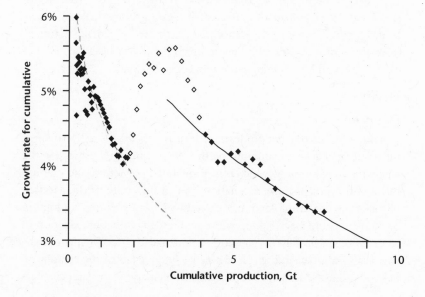

lived without power now want it. The utility has begun "load shedding" — regularly rotating ten percent of all consumers off the grid for two to four hours to keep the system operating.

One likely solution will be the building of more power plants, and many of these will almost certainly be coal-fired. This means more domestic demand for coal, and this will probably eat into export capacity. Other strategies are being considered as well — such as power rationing, nuclear power generation, solar- and wind-generated electricity, and building millions of solar collectors for heating domestic water.

Meanwhile, it may be unrealistic to expect South Africa to remain a reliable exporter of coal. Further, problems mentioned in the reports quoted above — declining resource quality, the aging and depletion of existing mines, and increasing transport challenges — suggest that growth in the nation's coal output may be difficult to achieve, and standard reserves figures may give an overly optimistic impression about the country's future coal prospects. Once again — as with nearly every nation surveyed so far — future production hinges on the development of lower-quality reserves in more distant regions, requiring the construction of new transport infrastructure at a time when transport costs are rising quickly.

During 2008, as coal prices rose and Europe began to turn back to coal for a variety of reasons (discussed below), exports from South Africa tripled. This had the effect of increasing domestic coal prices, contributing to the electricity shortages just noted. Gold and platinum mines were shut in January to avert a national power blackout. Higher power prices and continuing shortages seem inevitable.

Europe

Overview

In some respects this region deserves lengthy discussion, as Europe led the world in coal production during the 19th century and ushered in the Industrial Revolution — which transformed the economies and political fortunes not just of European nations but of the entire world. Modern history would have unfolded very differently if not for Europe's adoption of the flammable black stone, whose mining led to the introduction of labor unions; whose molecular constituents fed the development of the chemicals industry; and whose inherent energy enabled the creation of railroads and steamships. Europe is also emblematic of the later chapters

of coal's history: throughout the region, depletion is the underlying reason for the closure of countless coal mines and their related industries,
as well as the decline of miners' unions. Yet a long and detailed history
of Europe's transformation by coal, however fascinating and educative
(see Barbara Freese's *Coal: A Human History*[19]), would be out of place
here in a discussion of coal's future, because today Europe as a whole —
consisting of 27 countries, including the United Kingdom, Germany,
and France — is a relatively minor producer and has small, quickly dwin-
dling reserves to draw upon.

It would be impractical to discuss separately each of these 27 nations,
but two, Britain and Germany, must inevitably receive special attention.

The former has seen a nearly complete production cycle. British use
of coal for heating and cooking began in the 12th century following the
substantial deforestation of the countryside. By the 17th century, problems
with removing water from ever-deeper mineshafts led to the invention
of the first steam engine; and in the 18th century the need for better
means of removing coal from mines led to the adoption of steel rails. It
was inevitable that these two innovations would converge in the first
coal-burning steam railway (the Manchester to Leeds line), which
arrived in the early 19th century. Britain's coal miner unions led the
establishment of the world-wide labor movement; Britain's steamships,
burning British coal, led the process of globalization; and British mills
turned out manufactured products. In short, Britain was the first modern coal-powered economy.

Britain started out with more coal, in energy terms, than Saudi Arabia
has oil. However, by the 1970s, mines were being closed in large numbers,
leading to the wholesale loss of mining jobs. This provoked the greatest
labor conflict in British history, as the National Union of Mineworkers
fought to keep the mines open. The miner strikes were the defining
issue of the Thatcher regime: the "Iron Lady" eventually succeeded in
overcoming the union, and most of the mines were closed. With them
went a way of life, and entire towns in coalfield regions fell into economic and social ruin. This pivotal episode in the nation's social and
political history coincided with the opening of oil and gas production
from the North Sea: while Britain's coalfields were largely depleted, its
oil and gas fields would provide energy and income for the next two
decades (the nation's North Sea production peaked in 1999, and today
the United Kingdom is an importer of oil and gas as well as coal).

During the British coal decline from 1970 to the present, the number of jobs in the industry fell from 150,000 to fewer than 5,000[20]; today, there are only six deep mines still operating, although a few controversial open-cast coal pits are in the process of starting up. While a third of Britain's electricity still comes from burning coal, over half that coal is now purchased from South Africa, Australia, Colombia, and the United States.

German coal production also has a long tradition, and it played a pivotal role in the nation's rise to industrial prominence. German chemists were largely responsible for laying the foundations of the modern chemicals industry, using carbon compounds derived from coal. Coal also fueled the commercial and industrial rivalry between Britain and Germany that led to two World Wars (John Maynard Keynes would write that the German empire "was built more truly on coal and iron than on blood and iron"[21]). Throughout most of the 20th century, Germany was third in coal production behind the United States and Britain.

After World War II, coal yielded the energy for Germany's economic revival. The nation's coal produced both electricity and steel — the latter providing the basis for the German automobile industry. Hard coal production stood at about 40 million tons per year immediately following the war, but expanded quickly during the 1950s. Peak production was achieved in 1958 at 150 million tons, followed by a gradual decline. Hard coal production in 2005 was about 25 million tons.[22] Jobs in the coal mining industry fell from 339,000 in 1980 to 75,000 by 2000, with that number still declining.

Most of Germany's coal is soft lignite rather than hard anthracite or bituminous. The nation remains the world's largest brown coal producer, although production even of lignite is falling.

Other European nations' coal production deserves briefer mention.

France, never favored with coal resources on the scale of Britain or Germany, and an importer of coal throughout the 20th century, shut down its coal mining industry altogether in 2004. However, almost immediately plans were laid to start up an open-cast pit at Lucenay-les-Aix in the Burgundy region. Its coal, which is slated to become available starting in 2011, will fuel one of several new low-emissions power plants now on the drawing boards.[23]

Poland is ranked seventh in the world in coal production, although its mining industry is in decline. Total reserves of bituminous and sub-bituminous coal are estimated at 60 billion tons, with lignite reserves estimated at 14 billion tons.[24] Production of all categories has fallen steadily since the late 1980s. The collapse of the Communist regime played some part in the decline (many mines were closed in an economic rationalization program in the 1990s), but depletion of the highest-quality and most accessible seams is decisive and ongoing. Coal currently provides around 70 percent of Poland's total energy supply, including nearly all the nation's electricity and district heating. Coal production and use have led to severe environmental damage in Poland.

After World War II, the high costs of hard coal production in Germany, Italy, France, and the Benelux countries provided the initial impetus for the formation of a protected market within Europe. The result was the European Coal and Steel Community (ECSC), founded in 1952, which in turn laid the groundwork for the later European Union.

History of Reserves Estimates

As mentioned in Chapter 1, Britain's estimated coal R/P ratio started out at a healthy 900; the current figure currently stands at 9.[25]

Other European coal reserves downgrades have been equally dramatic. Germany's "proved recoverable coal reserves" were stated as being

Fig. 30

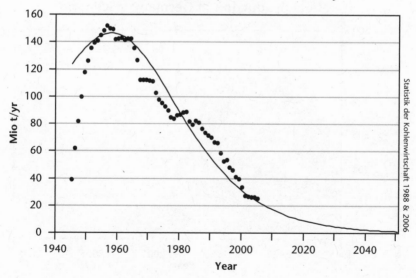

Hard coal production in Germany

Statistik der Kohlenwirtschaft 1988 & 2006

23 billion tons for many years until 2004, at which time the WEC 2004 report reclassified 99 percent of these proved reserves as speculative, and downgraded the total to 183 million tons.[26] The BP "Statistical Review" for 2008 states proved reserves of 152 million tons.[27]

Recent Studies

1

"Coal: Resources and Future Production" (Werner Zittel and Jörg Schindler, Energy Watch Group [EWG], March 2007)

This report discusses Germany in some detail, which is understandable given that its authors and publisher are German. Zittel and Schindler note that, "The dramatic downgrading of German hard coal reserves has not been explained and there has been no public debate of this fact," and suggest that, "The unexplained and far reaching downgradings of German hard coal reserves (and also resources) should be investigated and rediscussed in public because of their political implications."[28]

They note that, while Germany is the world's largest producer of lignite, responsible for about a third of world production,

the extraction effort rises continuously. This can be seen best [by] looking at the waste production which has steadily

Fig. 31

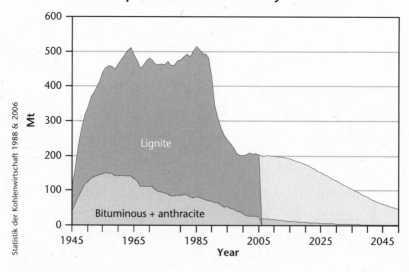

Coal production in Germany – Scenario

increased from two cubic meters per ton of lignite in 1950 to 5.5 cubic meters per ton of lignite in 2005. A more detailed analysis reveals that this trend can be observed in almost all producing regions with the only exception of the Rhineland. Lignite reserves also have been downgraded in the last years from 55 billion tons in 1990 to 43 billion tons in 2002 and recently to 6.6 billion tons in WEC 2004.

2

"The Future of Coal" (B. Kavalov and S.D. Peteves, Institute for Energy, 2007)

This report's purpose is to examine future coal availability from a European perspective, so it is not surprising that the authors provide a good overview of Europe's coal situation:

> Hard coal production in the EU generally suffers from largely depleted deposits, declining coal quality and excessively high production costs. Although indigenous lignite production is still cost-competitive with hard coal imports, the reserves of the main EU lignite producers are not plentiful and are being continuously depleted. ...At present, the prospects for European coal production are quite clear. Indigenous hard coal production in the EU will continue to decline for several reasons. Hard coal has been intensively mined in Europe for more than a century and the easier accessible deposits of

Fig. 32

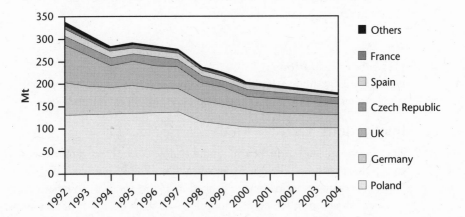

good quality have already been exploited. As hard coal in Europe can be recovered mainly from underground deposits, European coal miners are forced to go for deeper and more difficult to recover reserves of poorer quality, which increases costs. European indigenous hard coal production is two to three times more expensive than imported coal. Some EU countries have therefore ceased hard coal production. In the countries where hard coal production still exists (mainly for socio-economic reasons), it is heavily subsidised, but the subsidies are gradually being phased out.[29]

3

"Lignite and Hard Coal: Energy Suppliers for World Needs until the Year 2100 — An Outlook" (Thomas Thielemann, Sandro Schmidt, and J. Peter Gerling, German Federal Institute for Geosciences and Natural Resources [BGR], 2007). The BGR report offers no useful detail concerning future European coal production. The authors appear to assume that the EU will continue to import ever larger quantities, presumably from current sources (South Africa, and to a much lesser extent Australia, the United States, and South America).

4

"A Supply-Driven Forecast for the Future Global Coal Production" (Höök, Zittel, Schindler, and Aleklett; Uppsala Hydrocarbon Depletion Study Group).

No regional assessment is provided here, although Europe is mentioned in several places in the context of imports.

5

Hubbert linearization.
David Rutledge finds a Hubbert linearization trend for 21 billion tons of coal reserves remaining; reported reserves are 55 billion tons.[30]

Implications

The passage quoted from Peteves and Kavalov (above) well summarizes Europe's situation with regard to coal.

Coal consumption in Europe peaked in 1965, and it is now hard to foresee a situation in which consumption will grow to reach or surpass

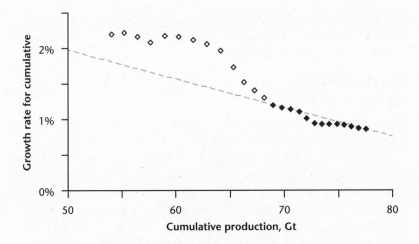

Fig. 33

that level. Consumption within Europe declined at a rapid rate from the late 1980s to the mid '90s, and the last eight to ten years has remained flat. Since EU coal production has continued to decline during recent years, the leveling off of consumption has resulted in increased reliance on coal imports.

As natural gas and nuclear power displaced coal for electric power generation, many coal mines within the EU were closed. While there may be some short-term possibility of re-invigorating the coal industries of Britain, Germany, and France, these can only be small-scale efforts because the most easily accessible and highest quality reserves are already depleted. Moreover, reopening a closed coal mine is likely to take an average of ten years. Clearly, therefore, if the region is to maintain its current level of dependence on coal for electricity generation and steel production, most of that coal will have to come from elsewhere.

But, in light of the other country assessments, the question arises: From where will those coal imports come? Competitive international demand from Asia is rising quickly, which means that Australia's export supplies may not be sufficient to meet demand for much longer; meanwhile other exporters face problems with transportation and the exhaustion of their own best sites. South America appears the most likely source for growth in exports to Europe. But if and when North America becomes a major importer, its demand may overwhelm what Colombia and Venezuela can offer, again leaving Europe bidding against other potential customers.

These problems may not become evident for several years. However, it would be prudent of European energy planners to assume much higher prices for coal in the future.

South America

Overview

South America's coal reserves and production are concentrated in two nations — Colombia and Venezuela.

Of the two, Colombia is currently by far the larger producer, mining 72 million tons in 2007, with plans to expand that amount to over 100 million tons in 2010.[31] Colombia's coal reserves account for around three-quarters of the region's total reserves and contain some of the highest-quality coals. Nearly all of production is exported. But substantial growth in exports will require port, road, and railway expansion, as well as an end to interference from militant groups (primarily FARC) that have a history of sabotaging coal operations.

Colombia's coal deposits are widespread, with significant deposits found in eight regions. The nation's geographic location is also of great significance, with easy access to markets in North America, Europe, and, via the Panama Canal, the Far East. About 95 percent of all Colombia's coal is bituminous, eight percent of which is coking quality. The remaining five percent of reserves consist of subbituminous coal.[32] No deposits of lignite have been identified. Colombian coal is generally of good quality, with low sulfur and ash content.

Venezuela produces 8.3 million tons of coal per year, while consuming only 100,000 tons per year domestically.[33] The Chavez government appears indecisive about whether to expand or eliminate coal mining, though currently environmental and indigenous concerns seem to be favored over export revenues. Venezuela has significant coal resources, with deposits located across the northern and northwestern parts of the country. Most of the recent mine developments have been concentrated within the Guasare Basin in the northwest of the country, close to the border with Colombia. As with Colombia, the quality of Venezuelan coal is good, with high energy content and few contaminants.

South America has only relatively recently become a significant producer and exporter of coal, and so its reserves are still largely intact, although the rapid expansion of Colombia's production has resulted in a shrinkage in the country's R/P ratio, from 177 at the end of 2000 to

112 at the end of 2005.[34] Exports from both nations are currently destined primarily for the United States and Europe. Venezuela seems to be the lowest-cost producer and exporter worldwide.

The primary impediments to further expansion of production and exports for both countries are the needs for sufficient foreign investment, and for the development of adequate export logistics and infrastructure (railways and ports). In the case of Venezuela, there are in addition governmental roadblocks to further exploiting production and export potentials.

Recent Studies

None of the recent studies finds substantial geological limits to increased production and exports from South America. The reports by Kavalov and Peteves[35] and Höök et al.[36] are the only ones to discuss the region in any detail. The latter report notes:

> Coal does not play a major role in Colombia's domestic energy production and its usage has been in decline since 1993. Only around 5.4% of the total coal production is consumed within the country, contributing by 8% to the total energy output of the country, and the rest of the coal is exported. Over 60% of the country's energy is derived from oil and gas. With increasing oil and gas prices it is possible that the domestic usage of coal is increased to free more oil and gas for export, or simply to reduce the cost of energy production. ...The production is estimated to increase to 70 Mt/year in 2020.

David Rutledge of Caltech finds no Hubbert linearization trend for the region and therefore adopts official reserves figures for the purposes of calculating global trends for future production.

Implications

South America may be the world's final coal frontier. Colombia's production is booming and government sources say the nation's exports, which have doubled in just five years, will continue to grow at ten percent per year. The primary factor likely to prevent such continued expansion is transport problems arising from higher diesel and bunker oil prices.

Indonesia
Overview

Since the early 1990s Indonesia has grown to become the world's second-largest coal exporter, with about 80 percent of produced coal being shipped abroad. Nearly all of this coal goes to Asia, with most currently being exported to Japan and Taiwan.

Coal mining for domestic consumption began here early in the 20th century, with peak production of some two Mt/year occurring in the early 1940s. However, the success of Indonesia's oil industry led to a reduction in coal output in the 1950s and '60s. Coal production increased again in the mid-1970s, and soon large resources of high-quality, mainly subbituminous coal were identified in the Kalimantan province on Borneo, the exploitation of which led to the ongoing export boom. Only a small proportion of Kalimantan's coal resource has been explored or assessed in detail.

A state-owned company, PT Batubara, produces most of the domestically-consumed coal from Sumatra, while foreign companies mine most of the Kalimantan coal for export.

Indonesian coal ranges from lignite to bituminous, with most of current production coming from low-cost, open-cast mines.

West Papua, the western half of New Guinea, has subbituminous and lignite deposits that have yet to be tapped, while Java's subbituminous seams are thin and can yield little coal on a commercial scale. South Sulawesi also has thin subbituminous seams that provide coal for local power production.

Recent Studies

1

"The Future of Coal" (B. Kavalov and S.D. Peteves, Institute for Energy, 2007).

Their assessment is that "…maintaining the present high output rates and export volumes may quite soon pose challenges." The authors point out that Indonesia's reserves are smaller than those of other major exporters, and that the recent production growth has begun to deplete the deposits of easily-accessible, high-grade coal. The report notes:

> As a result, the coal R/P ratio has almost halved over only six
> years — from 68 years at the end of 2000 to just 37 years at

the end of 2005. With these trends and with no additional investment in the coal sector, Indonesia would run out of economically recoverable (at current economic and operating conditions) reserves of coal much earlier than widely anticipated. On the other hand, the investment needed, if made, will almost certainly raise coal production costs, with a corresponding negative impact on the country's international competitiveness. Substantial improvements (and investments) are also urgently needed in the seaport infrastructure, which has recently become the main bottleneck for Indonesian coal exports. The availability of coal for export could come under further pressure from the widely expected significant increase in domestic consumption, along with economic growth.[37]

2

"A Supply-Driven Forecast for the Future Global Coal Production" (Höök, Zittel, Schindler, and Aleklett; Uppsala Hydrocarbon Depletion Study Group).
This report essentially concurs, noting:[38]

> The increasing domestic demand for electricity will make less coal available for export. Coal is also a vital substitute for oil and that can be seen in increased coal consumption in cement plants, petrochemical industries, pulp and paper factories and many others. The government has expressed an interest in reducing the dependence on oil and that may lead to export restrictions according to market analysts. ...Last year the domestic coal consumption increased by almost 18% and there is a growing discontent about the huge coal export from many groups. There are even plans about creating a "national reserve" for future generations, which means that untapped coal and metal reserves will be taken back by the government.

Implications

Indonesia is in the process of leaving OPEC because its declining oil production and growing domestic demand mean the country can no longer export petroleum. The country is also facing increasingly frequent power blackouts, and domestic coal demand is growing quickly.

Without sufficient electricity, the nation's economic development will stall or go into reverse. Under such circumstances, it is unrealistic to assume that the currently growing coal export trend will continue for long.

But the imperative to use more coal domestically and to decrease exports runs counter to the interests of regional coal importers India and China. Indonesia faces a metaphoric tug-of-war for its coal as shortages within East Asian and South Asian economies worsen, leading inevitably to higher coal prices that will impact Indonesia's economy as well as those of China and India.

Canada

Overview

Coal resources in Canada are concentrated in the provinces of British Columbia, Alberta, Saskatchewan, and, to a lesser extent, Nova Scotia. However, output from the last of these provinces is small and declining; the others show signs of increasing production.

The total production of Canadian coal was 66 Mt in 2004, and it has declined since then to 62.9 Mt in 2006.[39] Almost half of this production comes from Alberta, which produces slightly less than 30 Mt. Alberta contains 70 percent of Canada's total coal reserves. Nearly all production (98 percent) comes from surface mines; underground mines are very rare.

The nation exports almost half of its produced coal (28 Mt in 2006), and almost all of this is coking coal (only 1 Mt of steam coal was exported in 2006). Asia is the largest export market for Canadian coal (16 Mt in 2006), with the rest going mostly to Europe and South America.[40]

However, in 2006 Canada imported 21 Mt of coal — 17 Mt of steam coal for power plants in the eastern region and 4 Mt of coking coal for the steel industry. The United States supplied 18 Mt, and the rest came from Colombia, Venezuela, and Russia. The need for imported steam coal for power generation is due to geography: most production is in the west, where exports to Asia by ship are profitable; and most consumption is in the east, where imports by ship from South America are cheap.

A reserve assessment from 1925 estimated the "actual reserve," i.e., with seam width one foot and over and depths under 4,000 feet, as being 413,816 million metric tons with probable reserves of almost 800,000 million metric tons. Newer and better assessments have reduced this number significantly, and today only two percent of those "actual reserves" remain as proved as of the last assessment. In 2006, the reported proven coal reserves stated in the BP "Statistical Review of World Energy" were 6,578 Mt, with roughly half bituminous and the other half consisting of subbituminous and lignite.[41] However the last general assessment of Canada's coal reserves was conducted in 1987. Given recent reserves downgrades in other nations, this leaves room for skepticism about even the BP reserves number.

Recent Studies

Only one of the recent reports surveyed, "A Supply-Driven Forecast for the Future Global Coal Production" (Höök, Zittel, Schindler, and Aleklett; Uppsala Hydrocarbon Depletion Study Group), contains much detail about Canada:

> It is interesting to note that in terms of energy the production peaked in 1997 at 43 Mtoe [million tons oil equivalent] and has been in steady decline since then. Today it is 32.3 Mtoe. This can be explained by the large and rapid decrease in production of bituminous coal in Alberta. The production fell from 10,871 Mt in 1998 to 2,570 Mt in 2005. The production of subbituminous coal in Alberta increased until 1995 but has remained virtually constant since then. ...The collapse of the bituminous coal production from Alberta and the lack of expansion can be a sign of stagnation in the Canadian coal production.[42]

Implications

Canada is a major resource exporter to its neighbor to the south. Currently, 60 percent of Canadian natural gas production is piped to the United States, while 70 percent of Canada's homes are heated with gas. Under the terms of the NAFTA proportionality clause, Canada is obliged to continue exporting the same proportion of its gas in perpetuity. However, as Canada's gas production continues to decline, this will create obvious problems. If that clause continues to be honored, more domestically produced coal might be needed for heat and power.

Canada will likely remain a minor coal exporter in the near future, especially with regard to coking coal. But on balance and in the longer term, the nation's import requirements are likely to grow faster than its ability to export coal.

CHAPTER 6

Coal and Climate

RECENT REPORTS ON GLOBAL COAL RESERVES, surveyed in the previous chapters, generally point to the likelihood of supply limits appearing relatively soon — within the next two decades (a contrary view is represented solely by the BGR report[1]). According to this near-consensus, coal output in China, the world's foremost producer, could begin to decline within just a few years.

Since coal is the most significant source of human-generated greenhouse gas emissions, releasing about twice as much carbon dioxide per unit of energy produced as natural gas, the news that there may be much less coal available to be burned than commonly thought should be heartening to climate scientists and activists, and to policy makers and citizens concerned about the fate of the planet. Reduced estimates of future coal supplies should be factored into climate models — which typically assume that there is enough coal available to permit continued expansion of usage well into the next century.

At the same time, because global warming has emerged as the central environmental issue of our era, climate concerns will inevitably impact how much coal we continue to burn and how we burn it — whether these concerns come to be expressed through caps on emissions, carbon taxes, cancellation of orders for new coal-fired power plants, or the promotion of new carbon sequestration technologies. In any case, the coal industry will be — indeed, already is being — forced to change.

113

These two trends are surely destined to interact, and the uncertain result will shape climate and energy policy in the years to come.

A Tale of Two Crises

The idea that carbon dioxide emissions from burning fossil fuels might contribute to a greenhouse effect raising global temperatures was initially floated in the 1950s. The first evidence that global atmospheric CO_2 levels and global temperatures were both indeed increasing appeared in the early 1960s. The 1980s saw the first calls for international action to limit carbon emissions, with the first congressional hearings held in 1988. The initial report of the UN's International Panel on Climate Change (IPCC) was released in 1990.[2] In 1992, the Earth Summit in Rio de Janeiro produced the UN Framework Convention on Climate Change.[3] The third IPCC report, issued in 2001, stated that global warming, unprecedented since the end of the last Ice Age, is "very likely," with severe surprises possible.[4] By this time, debate among scientists over the question of whether human activities were contributing substantially to climate change had effectively ended. In 2003, numerous observations raised concern that the collapse of ice sheets in West Antarctica and Greenland could raise sea levels faster than most had believed possible. That same year, a deadly summer heat wave in Europe riveted public opinion on the issue. Work to retard emissions accelerated in Japan and Western Europe, and among US regional governments and corporations. In 2007, the fourth IPCC report warned that serious effects of warming have already become evident, and that the cost of reducing emissions would be far less than that for the damage they will cause.[5] In that same year, the north polar ice cap melted to such an extent that the northwest shipping passage was opened for the first time in history.

In short, over the past 50 years, anthropogenic climate change has evolved from a mere hypothesis to a robustly documented and widely-researched phenomenon; and from a concern on the part of just a few climate scientists to a center-stage issue dominating not just environmental studies, but economic planning and global politics as well.

While climate change is the greatest environmental crisis that humanity has ever faced, it is not the only serious challenge confronting us. Climate change is a "sink" problem — the result of dumping into the environment a waste product from the burning of fossil fuels. But there is a simultaneous "source" problem arising from the gradual depletion of the fuels we are burning.

At about the same time that the greenhouse hypothesis was first being proposed, geophysicist M. King Hubbert was publishing his first study on the phenomenon of oil depletion.[6] Previously, supply concerns about fossil fuels had centered on the question of when they would run out, and by most estimates that would not happen for a very long time. Hubbert reframed the discussion by pointing out that the rate of extraction of fossil fuels within any given region, or the world as a whole, will reach a maximum and begin to decline long before the resource is exhausted, and he suggested that it is this peaking of production that is critical for economic planning. By the mid-1970s, it was clear that US oil production had peaked and begun to decline, as Hubbert had estimated that it would. By this time, Hubbert and a few other petroleum geologists were forecasting a peak in global oil production around the turn of the century. In 1998, Colin Campbell and Jean Laherrère published a landmark article in *Scientific American* entitled "The End of Cheap Oil," in which they argued that oil reserves in the Middle East were overstated, and that world petroleum production would hit its maximum before 2010.[7] At that time, the world oil price was hovering in the range of $12 per barrel. By 2000, British oil production from the North Sea had begun to fall, and it was apparent that about half the world's other oil producing nations were also in plateau or decline. In 2005, a study for the US Department of Energy concluded that the world oil production peak would have "unprecedented" social, economic, and political consequences.[8] In 2008, the International Energy Agency warned of a severe mismatch between world petroleum supply and demand in the years immediately ahead.[9] By this time, oil's price had risen to nearly $150 a barrel, and soaring fuel costs were severely impacting the automobile industry, the airline industry, the trucking industry, and tourism.

Because natural gas and coal are also non-renewable, it is inevitable that depletion will result in peaks and declines of output for these fuels as well. However, studies of Peak Gas and Peak Coal have lagged behind those of Peak Oil. While some awareness of coal limits can be traced back at least to the work of Andrew Crichton in 1948,[10] the discussion of Peak Coal really started with the appearance of reports from the Energy Watch Group[11] and the National Academy of Sciences,[12] both in

2007. A report from the Energy Watch Group on global natural gas supplies is due in 2009.

Meanwhile, although the timing of the global oil, gas, and coal production peaks is still controversial, the peaking concept has become sufficiently accepted that its significance for climate change has begun to be explored.

Climate Models and Fossil Fuel Supplies

Models for future impacts of climate change must be based on two essential parameters: the quantity of future greenhouse gas emissions that can reasonably be anticipated; and the sensitivity of the climate to added increments of atmospheric greenhouse gases. Both of these parameters are subject to ongoing research and revision.

In its Special Reports on Emissions Scenarios (SRES),[13] the International Panel on Climate Change has published a series of 40 scenarios for fossil fuel's contribution to future climate change. The latest of these reports, in 2007, was a multi-year effort involving more than 1,000 authors and more then 1,000 reviewers. In the assessment modeling, limitations in fossil-fuel supplies are not considered critically. For example, in 17 of the scenarios, world oil production is higher in 2100 than it was in 2000 — a situation not considered likely even by OPEC.

In 1996, the European Environment Council said that the global average surface temperature increase should be held to a maximum of two degrees C above pre-industrial levels, and that to accomplish this the atmospheric concentration of carbon dioxide will have to be stabilized at 550 parts per million (ppm)[14] (the pre-industrial level was 280 ppm and the current concentration is close to 390 ppm, though the addition of other greenhouse gases raises the figure to the equivalent of 440 to 450 ppm of CO_2[15]). The European Union has more recently adopted a target of 450 ppm of CO_2, in line with recommendations from climate scientists.

However, the IPCC scenarios suggest that if fossil fuel consumption continues to increase throughout the century, CO_2 concentrations could reach a staggering 960 ppm by 2100, which would result in six or more degrees of warming, tilting the global climate into an entirely new regime and triggering an endless list of environmental horrors.

Jean Laherrère was an early critic of the SRES, arguing in 2001 that failure to make realistic estimates of fossil fuel supplies and the inclusion of false supply numbers in climate models was resulting in highly unrealistic estimates of future atmospheric CO_2 concentrations, future temperature increases, and future effects on climate, ocean levels, and so on.[16]

In April 2008, James E. Hansen, head of the NASA Goddard Institute for Space Studies in New York City, who has arguably done more than any other scientist in recent years to both assess and publicize the likely impacts of climate change, co-authored an important paper (together with P.A. Kharecha of the Columbia University Earth Institute) that discusses fossil fuel supply limits.[17] These authors explicitly mention Peak Oil, and stress that, "[I]t is important to estimate expected atmospheric CO_2 levels for realistic estimates of fossil fuel reserves and to determine how the CO_2 level depends upon possible constraints on coal use."

In this paper, "Implications of 'Peak Oil' for Atmospheric CO_2 and Climate," Kharecha and Hansen discuss five scenarios. In their "Business as Usual" (BAU) base case, "Peak oil emission ... occurs in 2016 ± 2 yr, peak gas in 2026 ± 2 yr, and peak coal in 2077 ± 2 yr." Most of the IPCC scenarios show far higher CO_2 concentrations than Kharecha and Hansen's BAU scenario.

The authors also discuss a "Coal Phase-out" scenario that "moves peak coal up to 2022." This second scenario "is meant to approximate a situation in which developed countries freeze their CO_2 emissions from coal by 2012 and a decade later developing countries similarly halt increases in coal emissions." This Coal Phase-out scenario shows a peak of atmospheric CO_2 concentrations at about 445 ppm in 2046.

One message from the paper is that climate mitigation efforts should not focus so much on reducing oil and gas demand, as these fuels are supply-limited. Rather, they should concentrate on reducing the exploitation of coal and unconventional fossil fuels, since these are demand- rather than supply-limited for the time being. This message is more explicit in Hansen's June 23, 2008 congressional testimony:

> Phase out of coal use except where the carbon is captured and stored below ground is the primary requirement for solving global warming. Oil is used in vehicles where it is impractical to capture the carbon. But oil is running out. To preserve our planet we must also ensure that the next mobile energy source is not obtained by squeezing oil from coal.[18]

Kharecha and Hansen cite the NRC report of 2007[19] and suggest, "[E]ven if coal reserves are much lower than historically assumed ... there is surely enough coal to take the world past 450 ppm CO_2 without mitigation efforts such as those described here." EWG, Höök et al., Laherrère, and Rutledge all show future coal supply limits that are roughly in accord with Kharecha and Hansen's Coal Phase-out scenario, and that appear to achieve a target of approximately 450 ppm CO_2.

A month after the release of the Kharecha and Hansen paper, Kjell Aleklett, professor of Physics at Uppsala University and President of the Association for the Study of Peak Oil (ASPO), published an article provocatively titled, "Global Warming Exaggerated, Insufficient Oil, Natural Gas and Coal" (2007).[20] Aleklett's main purpose was to take the IPCC to task:

> The sum of all fossil resources that the industry considers available is presented annually in BP Statistical Review. According to this rather optimistic estimate, the total energy of all oil, natural gas and coal amounts to 36 Zeta joules (ZJ), a gigantic amount of energy. This is more than what our research group considers likely, but it is still less than what the [SRES] scenario families A1, A2, B1 and B2 require. ...Up to 2100, IPCC prognosticates that A2 will need between 70 and 90 ZJ, that is, twice as much as the industry believes is available. ...We need a new assessment of future temperature increases based on a realistic consumption of oil, natural gas and coal.

David Rutledge published his paper, "The Coal Question and Climate Change," in June 2007. In it, he compared the results of Hubbert linearization modeling of future coal production with the IPCC models.[21] He concluded, "Our Producer-Limited Profile has future fossil-fuel production that is lower than all 40 of the IPCC scenarios, so it seems that producer limitations could provide useful constraints in climate modeling." More specifically, "The Producer-Limited Profile gives a peak of 460 ppm in 2070" — which is only marginally above the widely accepted target of 450 ppm. The implication is clear: sufficient greenhouse gas reductions will be accomplished by fossil fuel depletion alone, without any need for carbon emissions regulatory policy.

In short, the implication of the latest research might appear to be that Peak Oil, Peak Gas, and Peak Coal will together solve the problem of global Climate Change, without need for intervention by policy makers.

However, this could be a dangerously premature conclusion.

Climate Sensitivity

Recall that climate models depend not only on future carbon emissions (which are contingent, as we have just seen, on fossil fuel supplies as well as on energy policy) but also on climate sensitivity. How will the global climate respond to a given additional increment of carbon dioxide? In general, as observations of impacts from climate change are being logged, they are tending to show that past assumptions about climate sensitivity have, if anything, been too timid and conservative.

Most climate sensitivity models are now being seen as subject to three problems. First, they tend to assume a linear relationship between atmospheric greenhouse gas concentrations and global temperature increase, whereas there is mounting evidence that the relationship is actually nonlinear. Second, they tend to assume a linear relationship between global temperature increase and actual impacts to ecosystems and human society, whereas there is mounting evidence that this relationship is also nonlinear. Third, such models have created a questionable basis for policy: it has been widely accepted that a future temperature increase of two degrees C (which is assumed to be tied to a greenhouse gas concentration of 450 ppm) must be our target limit; above this increase, changes to the climate will be catastrophic, irreversible, and unacceptable. In fact, we may already be seeing degrees of change that are catastrophic, effectively irreversible, and unacceptable.

Nonlinearity in the relationship between greenhouse gases and temperature increase was demonstrated by a 2005 study by researchers at the Potsdam Institute for Climate Impact in Germany, which concluded that — to keep the temperature from increasing more than two degrees C — the atmospheric concentration of greenhouse gases would need to be stabilized at then-current levels (i.e., 380 ppm).[22] Among other things, the study pointed out that the biosphere's ability to absorb carbon is being reduced by human activity, and this must be factored into the equations; by 2030, this carbon-absorbing ability will have been reduced from the current 4 billion tons per year to 2.7 billion tons.

Nonlinearity of the consequences of global warming is illustrated by several potential self-reinforcing feedback mechanisms that, if triggered, could result in effects spiraling far out of human control. Perhaps the scariest of these has to do with the vast amounts of methane (a greenhouse gas over 20 times more potent than carbon dioxide) locked in the ocean floor and in the frozen soils of Siberia, Northern Europe, and North America. Climate warming could trigger a rapid thawing that would release billions of tons of this stored methane into the atmosphere. More methane in the atmosphere would create more warming, which would release still more methane. The ultimate consequence might be the tipping of the planet into a new climate regime so different from the current one that many higher life forms (including humans) might find survival difficult or impossible.

The inadequacy of policies that use 450 ppm and a two degree C average global temperature increase as targets or limits is illustrated by evidence that catastrophic climate change has already been set in motion on the basis of a mere one degree C global temperature rise. For example: recent observations have established that oceans are absorbing increasing amounts of carbon dioxide from the atmosphere, resulting in their gradual acidification.[23] In the last two centuries, the oceans have absorbed roughly half of the amount of CO_2 emitted by fossil fuel use and cement production. This has caused ocean pH to fall. Ocean acidity will be devastating to the marine environment within a short period of time — tens of years instead of hundreds of years. Seawater undersaturated in calcium carbonate will make it difficult for shelled organisms to create skeletons and shells. These organisms form an essential link in the aquatic food chain; thus, all life in the seas will be impacted. Given that the oceans have already absorbed a substantial amount of carbon dioxide, we are already committed to an irreversible amount of ocean acidification. It is likely that rebalancing the ocean pH will take thousands, or even hundreds of thousands, of years.

Ocean acidification again illustrates the disturbing fact that very little about "global warming" is simple or linear. Instead, the consequences of greenhouse gas emissions are complex, mutually interacting, and far-reaching. Rather than merely having to accustom ourselves to winters and summers a degree or two hotter, we will see far more severe storms of all kinds, as well as rising sea levels, collapsing ecosystems, disease outbreaks, species extinctions, profound challenges to agricultural production, and more. We may already have committed ourselves to centuries of overwhelming environmental damage.

If we are already seeing fundamental changes to the world's oceanic food chain, to the Arctic sea ice, and to glaciers that feed some of the world's most important river systems, can we afford to commit ourselves to still higher atmospheric greenhouse gas concentrations (450 ppm instead of the current 390), and to a two degree C temperature increase above pre-industrial levels, instead of the single degree that has already produced these impacts?

In a recent paper, "Target Atmospheric CO_2: Where Should Humanity Aim?", James Hansen, along with nine co-authors, questioned the 450 ppm target and suggested a new one:[24]

> Our current analysis suggests that humanity must aim for an even lower level of GHGs. Paleoclimate data and ongoing global changes indicate that "slow" climate feedback processes not included in most climate models, such as ice sheet disintegration, vegetation migration, and GHG release from soils, tundra or ocean sediments, may begin to come into play on time scales as short as centuries or less. Rapid on-going Climate Changes and realization that Earth is out of energy balance, implying that more warming is "in the pipeline," add urgency to investigation of the dangerous level of GHGs. ...We use paleoclimate data to show that long-term climate has high sensitivity to climate forcings and that the present global mean CO_2, 385 ppm, is already in the dangerous zone. ...Ongoing Arctic and ice sheet changes, examples of rapid paleoclimate change, and other criteria cited above all drive us to consider scenarios that bring CO_2 more rapidly back to 350 ppm or less.

On the basis of this article and the recent findings that prompted it, climate activists such as Bill McKibben and George Monbiot have also begun to call for more stringent targets — 350 ppm target for atmospheric CO_2 concentrations and a 100 percent reduction in carbon emissions by 2050.[25]

This is a far more rapid and drastic reduction in carbon emissions than can be achieved by fossil fuel resource depletion alone.

Further, relying on fossil fuel depletion to safeguard the world's climate would entail a serious risk: What if the new, lower estimates of coal reserves turn out to be wrong? Clearly, the world's oil and coal reserves are a mere fraction of total resources. If somehow a way were found to transform a significant portion of remaining resources into reserves, this could entail a significant increase in atmospheric carbon emissions.

This risk also extends to unconventional fossil fuels such as tar sands, shale oil, and methane hydrates. The potential for the development of these resources is often overstated, since current technology will permit only a very slow extraction rate for tar sands and perhaps no commercial extraction at all of oil shale and methane hydrates. Nevertheless, there is always the possibility that new technologies will enable their exploitation on a wide scale. Without a stringent emissions policy in place, the consequences for the global climate would be profound.

In general, human society faces a conundrum: unless non-fossil sources of energy are developed quickly, or unless society finds a way to operate with much less energy, the depletion of higher-quality fuels (natural gas and oil) will mean that efforts to obtain more energy will entail burning ever dirtier fuels, and doing so in proportionally larger quantities in order to derive equivalent amounts of energy.

Therefore, to the question, "Will coal, oil, and gas depletion solve climate change?", the answer is an unequivocal *no*.

Will Climate Change Solve Peak Coal?

If some Peak Oil-Coal-Gas analysts suggest that depletion will stop climate change, climate activists look at the matter the other way around. While peaks and declines in the production of fossil fuels will undoubtedly have enormous societal consequences, these nevertheless pale compared to the potential ecological effects of climate change. Peak Oil may result in the collapse of the global economy; climate change could do so as well, while also devastating Earth's ecosystems in a way that would require millennia, perhaps millions of years, for planetary recovery.

But if we proactively deal with climate change by reducing fossil fuel consumption, the result will obviously be a reduction in our dependence on fossil fuels — and therefore a solution to the problems of Peak Oil, Gas, and Coal. Therefore, all that is needed is a clear, sustained, and vigorous policy focus on reducing greenhouse gas emissions by reducing fossil fuel consumption.

There is some evidence to support this argument. Efforts to reduce carbon emissions are already having an impact on the coal industry, primarily in the United States and Europe (though not nearly to the same degree in China and India). In the United States, nearly 90 percent of all new coal power plant projects proposed between 2000 and 2006 were delayed or cancelled, according to an October 2007 report by the US Department of Energy[26] — many over concerns about future carbon emissions regulations. Of 151 proposals for new plants submitted in early 2007, almost half had been dropped by year's end, many blocked by state governments or delayed by court challenges. In July 2008, a judge in Georgia threw out an air pollution permit for a new coal-fired power plant because the permit did not set limits on carbon dioxide emissions.[27] In Europe new coal plants are faring better, but only because higher-efficiency power plants are being proposed.

Climate mitigation efforts typically center on "cap and trade" (or "cap and dividend" or "cap and share" — alternative regimes being proposed by a number of economic equity activists), or on carbon taxes. Any of these policies to restrict carbon emissions will inevitably reduce fossil fuel consumption, impacting coal more than other fuels simply because of coal's higher carbon content. While future coal-burning power plants could be constructed to capture carbon, which could then be permanently sequestered underground (a technology discussed in the next chapter), over the short term, reducing carbon emissions simply means using less coal.

If these efforts were to pick up speed, they would reduce demand for coal (and other fossil fuels), thus heading off shortages and keeping prices low.

But will climate concerns succeed in driving policy in the face of energy scarcity? Currently, global coal consumption is still growing — faster, indeed, than the consumption of any other energy resource. Can nations experiencing shortages of oil and battered by high energy prices be persuaded to forgo the still relatively cheap energy from coal in order to avert environmental consequences for future generations?

From the perspective of climate scientists and activists, there can be no question: whatever short-term economic pain society may experience as a result of deliberately reducing fossil fuel consumption can hardly be compared with the overwhelming catastrophe that unbridled climate change would bring. However, policy makers may look at the evidence through an entirely different lens — one that discounts the future in favor of the present.

In his book *Material Concerns: Pollution, Profit and Quality of Life*, Professor of Sustainable Development and UK government advisor Tim Jackson describes it this way:[28]

> [F]uture costs and benefits are taken to have a lower value than present costs and benefits. We can think of the *discount* rate as the rate of return which is required on capital invested by the company. The higher the discount rate, the lower the value of future costs against present costs. For example, a cost of $200,000 which occurs twenty years in the future has a net present value of $44,000 at 5 percent and $10,400 at 10 percent discount rate. The further into the future costs and benefits arise, the lower their value compared with present costs and benefits.

Hagens argues that discount rates are based in fundamental human psychology, and perhaps even hardwired into our genes and nervous systems. We instinctively value the concrete present over the likely or hypothesized future.

The relevance for climate change — and other environmental issues, such as resource depletion — is clear: we tend to discount future *costs* (such as the impact of melting glaciers) just as we do future profits. Thus, asking society to endure present pain in order to avert more widespread suffering in the future is problematic. The present pain must be minor, and the future suffering profound and credible, in order to persuade us to action.

In the early years of the decade, as the global economy was booming, policy makers in many nations gave considerable attention to climate change. Heads of state conferred, strategies were debated, and agreements were forged. More recently, as energy scarcity crippled national economies with pain that was palpable and systemic, a tendency to discount the future costs of climate change in favor of satisfying the immediate demand for fuel, no matter how carbon-intensive it may be, began to appear.

In Europe, while top climate experts offer ever-shriller warnings about the effects of carbon emissions, Italy is planning to increase its reliance on coal from 14 percent of total energy to 33 percent. Throughout the continent, about 50 new coal-fired power stations are being planned for the next five years. The driver for this new coal boom is unequivocally clear: higher natural gas prices. In Germany, 27 new coal plants are planned by 2020, many fueled by lignite — which can produce a ton of carbon emissions for every ton of coal burned.[29]

In the United States, despite the cancellation of so many new coal plants in recent years, the National Mining Association projects that about 54 percent of the nation's electric power will be coal-fired by 2030, up from the current 48 percent.[30]

Depletion defeats climate policy in other ways. Carbon taxes become a harder policy to sell as energy prices climb; coal cutbacks are more difficult to make when natural gas is getting more expensive and electricity grids are browning out; and using coal to make liquid fuels starts to look attractive as diesel prices escalate.

Will efforts to address climate change solve the economic problems arising from coal, oil, and gas depletion and increasing scarcity? It is possible in principle, but in reality the stronger likelihood is that energy scarcity will rivet the attention of policy makers and private citizens alike because it is an immediate and unavoidable crisis. The result: as scarcity deepens, support for climate policy may fade even as climate impacts worsen.

A Combined Approach

Clearly, the world needs energy policies that successfully address both climate change and fuel scarcity. Such policies are likely to be devised and implemented only if both crises are acknowledged and taken into account in a strategically sensible way.

If policy makers focus only on one of these problems, some of the strategies they are likely to promote could simply exacerbate the other crisis. For example, some actions that might help reduce the impact of Peak Oil — such as exploitation of tar sands or oil shale, or the conversion of coal to a liquid fuel — will result in an increase in carbon emissions. On the other hand, some actions aimed to help reduce carbon emissions — such as carbon sequestration or carbon taxes — will make energy more expensive, which, in a situation of energy scarcity and high prices, may be politically problematic.

However, many policies will help with both problems — including any effort to develop renewable energy sources or to reduce energy consumption.

For strategic purposes, it is important to understand our human tendency to discount future problems. We must assess which threats will come soonest, and make sure that our sometimes frantic efforts to respond to these immediate necessities do not exacerbate problems that will show up later. Peak Oil is clearly the most immediate energy and resource supply threat that policy makers must deal with. Peak Coal and climate change may seem comparatively distant. But all must be taken seriously if we are to do any better than merely to lurch from crisis to crisis, with each new one worse than the last.

If energy scarcity forces policy changes before climate fears can do so, then perhaps world leaders will find that it makes more sense to ration

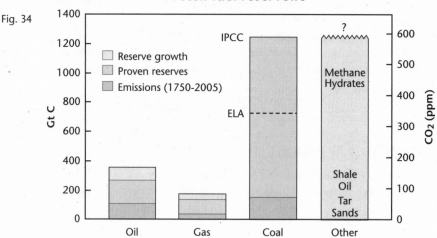

Fig. 34

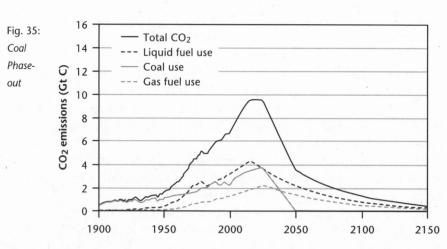

Fig. 35:
Coal
Phase-
out

fuels themselves, rather than the emissions they produce. In any case, it will help everyone concerned to have a clear idea of the ultimate extent of coal, oil, and natural gas reserves and future production, as well as a realistic understanding of the environmental and economic consequences of continuing to burn fossil fuels. Otherwise, the policies pursued are likely to be ineffective, counterproductive, and inconsistent.

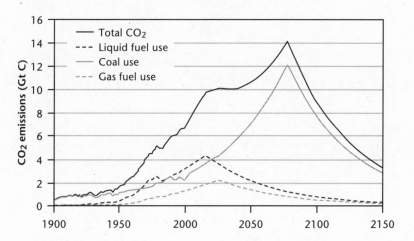

Fig. 36:
Business as Usual

CHAPTER

7

New Coal Technologies

FOR COAL, THE FUTURE of both extraction and consumption depends on new technology. If successfully deployed, innovative technologies could enable the use of coal that cannot be mined by gasifying it underground; they could reduce coal's carbon emissions; or they could allow coal to take the place of natural gas or petroleum. Without these technologies, coal simply may not have much of a future. Are these technologies close to development? Are they economical? Will they work?

The technologies discussed in this chapter go by some rather unwieldy names, and so we shall call them by their customary acronyms: coal-to-liquids (CTL), Underground Coal Gasification (UCG), Integrated Gasification Combined Cycle (IGCC), and Carbon Capture and Storage (CCS).

Many energy experts believe that these technologies may largely define the world's energy path for the next few decades.

Integrated Gasification Combined Cycle (IGCC)

Among these technologies, gasification of coal is a recurring theme. Once coal is reduced to a gas, the gas can be burned to turn a turbine to generate electricity, or it can be made into a liquid fuel, various useful chemicals, or fertilizers. Carbon can be stripped from the gas and buried, thus reducing the climate impact from burning coal.

In most instances (with the exception of UCG), gasification is accomplished in — of all things — a gasifier, into which coal, water, and air are fed. Heat and pressure reduce the coal to "synthesis gas" or "syngas" — a mixture of carbon monoxide and hydrogen, along with solid waste byproducts consisting of ash and slag, which can be used in making concrete or roadbeds.

The hot syngas must then be cleansed of contaminants (including hydrogen sulfide, ammonia, mercury, and particulates) via heat exchangers, particulate filters, and quench chambers, which also cool the syngas to room temperature. A bed of charcoal captures over 90 percent of the syngas mercury (used charcoal is sent to a hazardous-waste landfill). Finally, sulfur impurities are separated out in acid gas removal units, which produce sulfuric acid or elemental sulfur that can be sold as byproducts.

An IGCC power plant then uses the syngas the way most coal is already used — to make electricity. The plant is called "Integrated" because syngas is produced in the plant itself, in a way that optimizes the product for its intended purpose (i.e., to power a turbine generator). The "Combined Cycle" in the name refers to the use of gas to power a turbine generator whose waste heat is passed to a steam turbine system. This way, the energy of the syngas is used as fully and efficiently as possible.

Efficiency is important not only for its own sake (energy efficiency is almost always a good thing), but also because it is necessary from a cost standpoint: gasifying the coal is expensive, so if IGCC electricity is to be cost-competitive, savings must come from efficiency advantages elsewhere in the process. (It is also possible to capture waste heat from a conventional coal power plant; this is often done simply by piping hot air to commercial and residential buildings. The process, whether it uses coal or some other fuel, is called "cogeneration," or "combined heat and power" [CHP].)

The advantages of IGCC over conventional coal power plants include greater thermal efficiency (IGCC power plants use less coal and produce much lower emissions of carbon dioxide and other pollutants than conventional power plants) plus product flexibility: coal gasification enables the production of not only electricity, but a range of chemicals and by-products for industrial use (including transport fuels — see CTL below). IGCC is sometimes mentioned as a pathway to a hydrogen-centered economy, since syngas is a source of hydrogen. Last, but hardly least, carbon capture and storage is much easier and cheaper in IGCC plants than in regular coal power plants.

As of 2008 there are only two IGCC plants operating in the United States, following the closure of one of the three demonstration plants constructed in the 1990s with the help of the Department of Energy Clean Coal Demonstration Project[1] (Wabash River Power Station in West Terre Haute, Indiana; Polk Power Station in Tampa, Florida; and Piñon Pine in Reno, Nevada). The Reno demonstration project failed when researchers found that then-current IGCC technology would not work at more than 300 feet (100 meters) above sea level because reduced atmospheric pressure at higher elevations created inefficiencies in the gasification process.

These first-generation IGCC plants generated less air pollution than regular coal power stations, but polluted water to a greater degree.

New-generation IGCC power plants in the United States are in the planning and approval process and are being developed by Excelsior Energy, AEP, Duke Energy, and Southern Company. If successfully completed, these are expected to come on line between 2012 and 2020.

The principal drawback of IGCC technology is its high cost. The US Department of Energy has estimated a cost of $1,491 per kilowatt (kW) of installed capacity in 2005 dollars for an IGCC plant, versus $1,290 for a conventional pulverized coal station.[2] However, the example of Excelsior Energy's Mesaba project (an IGCC plant in northern Minnesota slated to begin operation in 2012) suggests that a realistic figure might be in excess of $3,600 per kW. Operating costs are also high, likely to be up to double those of a conventional coal plant, even without CCS technology being added on. Further, the Minnesota Department of Commerce has concluded that the pollution profile of the proposed Mesaba plant would not be substantially better than that of a standard coal power plant.[3] An analysis of the proposal for an IGCC plant in Delaware by Delmarva and a state consultant arrived at essentially the same conclusions.

The high-cost hurdle is perhaps reflected in the recent US Government revocation of support for its FutureGen low emissions coal gasification project, developed as a public-private partnership between the US Department of Energy and a non-profit consortium of 12 American and international energy companies.[4] (The proposed IGCC plant site at Mattoon, Illinois, had been selected after a hard-fought battle with two sites in Texas and another in Illinois.)

Other countries have had somewhat better experiences with the technology. The 250 MW Buggenum plant in the Netherlands currently uses about 30 percent biomass feedstock as a supplement to coal (the Dutch government pays the plant's owner, Nuon, an incentive fee to use the biomass). Nuon is currently building another 1300 MW IGCC plant that will be commissioned in 2011.[5] Other refinery-based IGCC plants are operating in Puertollano, Spain (operated by Elcogas, startup in 1998) and Vresova in the Czech Republic (operated by Sokolovska Uhelna, startup in 1996); as well as several in Italy and Germany, and one in Portugal. More European IGCC power plants are being planned by Centrica in the United Kingdom, and by E.ON and RWE in Germany.

Japan has been operating an IGCC pilot plant since the early 1990s and commissioned a new demonstration plant in Nakano in 2007.

While the high cost of IGCC is the biggest obstacle to its wider adoption, most energy company executives recognize that carbon regulation is coming soon. Adding carbon capture equipment to an IGCC plant would increase the cost of its electricity by approximately 30 percent — slightly less that it would for a natural gas plant and less than half the price increase for a pulverized coal power plant. This potential for cheaper carbon capture leads many analysts to view IGCC as an attractive choice to keep coal cost-competitive in a carbon-regulated world.

Nevertheless, there is no getting around the fact that the price of IGCC electricity is higher than electricity from a conventional coal plant, and adding carbon capture will increase that price still further. The future of IGCC hinges on these questions: Which will be a bigger issue, affordability of energy or carbon neutrality? Will carbon capture work as planned? Will it be scaleable? And when will it be ready for wide deployment? If energy affordability turns out to be society's more important concern, or if CCS technology cannot be developed successfully and soon, the case for IGCC falls apart.

Coal-to-Liquids

In the last few years, as world oil prices gyrated upward to the point of seriously imperiling the world economy, farmers, truckers, airlines, and ordinary commuters all felt the effects. The world's transport infrastructure is 95 percent dependent on liquid fuels; with time and investment, gasoline-powered cars can be replaced with electric vehicles, but for air travel, trucking, and shipping there are currently no large-scale alternatives to petroleum-based fuels.

One possible solution would be to turn coal into a synthetic liquid fuel to replace petroleum. Coal, after all, is still cheap and abundant, and the technology for liquefying it already exists.

The basic process for CTL was developed at the beginning of the 20th century and was used by Germany during World War II when the Allies cut off access to petroleum imports. At its peak output period in 1944, Germany produced about 125,000 barrels of synthetic fuel daily from 25 CTL plants, meeting 90 percent of the nation's needs. South Africa's apartheid regime revived the process during the 1980s, when trade embargoes made oil scarce for that nation. The South African company Sasol is currently the world's largest commercial producer of liquid fuels from coal, making about 150,000 barrels per day.

The fact that CTL has been developed for use only twice, and both times in a situation where access to regular petroleum had been cut off, suggests that the economics are unfavorable. An April 2008 article in *Oil and Gas Journal* ("GTL, CTL Finding Roles in Global Energy Supply") noted that, based on Sasol's experience, it currently costs about $67 to $82 to make a barrel of CTL fuel, depending on coal and water prices.[6] Given that oil prices were recently far above that range, the growth of interest in CTL is predictable. But building coal liquefaction plants is also costly — about $25,000 per barrel of installed production capacity as of 2005, according to the National Academies,[7] although projects currently under construction appear to be aiming to spend up to $120,000 per barrel of capacity.[8]

Often, discussions about the economics of CTL turn on the question: How high does the oil price have to rise in order for CTL to be competitive? Back in 2006, one source calculated that CTL could compete with $40 oil.[9] But since then, as oil prices surpassed that level, rising infrastructure costs have marked up the estimated price tag for producing CTL fuels. This ratcheting effect will likely continue: when the price of oil goes up, the cost of building and running CTL plants will rise as well. Ongoing hikes in the price of coal also must be factored in. Altogether, then, the cost-competitiveness of CTL cannot be defined by a couple of static numbers; the break-even price is a moving target — and usually it moves the wrong way to make this technology attractive.

From an energy standpoint, the process only makes sense if liquid fuels are at a premium for qualities other than their energy content, because coal turned into electricity at high efficiency will power electric vehicles three times as far as liquid fuel made from an equivalent amount of coal will push a combustion engine vehicle.

Since large or swift electric aircraft are impracticable, the aviation industry (including military aviation) will need liquid fuels even after those fuels' prices have risen far above those of other energy sources on a per-BTU basis, so this is likely a long-term market for CTL fuels.

Two different CTL technologies are being considered. The process used by the Nazis and by Sasol is called *indirect CTL;* it entails gasifying the coal at high pressure and temperature, then using the Fischer-Tropsch process to synthesize a liquid fuel from the syngas. This first process is sometimes also known as "coal Gas-to-Liquids" or "coal GTL." Shenhua in China is working on a different process, *direct CTL,* that bypasses the gasification stage.

One drawback for both processes is the fact that CTL emits carbon. In the case of indirect CTL, much of the carbon in the coal could be captured at the gasification stage and then sequestered, although this would add significantly to the already high cost of the finished fuel. However, even if this were done, CO_2 would still be emitted when the liquid fuel is burned.

A 2007 US Government Accountability Office (GAO) study on Peak Oil identified significant problems with CTL:

> This fuel is commercially produced outside the United States, but none of the production facilities are considered profitable. DOE reported that high capital investments — both in money and time — deter the commercial development of coal GTL in the United States. Specifically, DOE estimates that construction of a coal GTL conversion plant could cost up to $3.5 billion and would require at least 5 to 6 years to construct. Furthermore, potential investors are deterred from this investment because of the risks associated with the lengthy, uncertain, and costly regulatory process required to build such a facility. An expert at DOE also expressed concern that the infrastructure required to produce or transport coal may be insufficient. For example, the rail network for

transporting western coal is already operating at full capacity and, owing to safety and environmental concerns, there is significant uncertainty about the feasibility of expanding the production capabilities of eastern coal mines.[10]

China stands poised to invest in CTL technology soonest and on the largest scale (see Chapter 3), though many proposed plants have recently been canceled due to high projected costs. In Canada, Alter NRG Corp has proposed a CTL project that will use the company's coal reserves in the Fox Creek area of Alberta as a feedstock to produce synthetic diesel fuel and naphtha. The project, with a targeted production capacity of 40,000 barrels per day, will require an investment of approximately C$4.5 billion.[11]

In the United States, the Air Force is offering a base in Montana as a pilot site for a CTL project. Funding will come from the private sector, but the Air Force will guarantee purchase of the fuel at a price that guarantees a profit. The Defense Department is working on plans to eventually fuel much of the Air Force fleet with a mixture of CTL fuel and conventional kerosene, and it has already tested several planes on synthetic fuels. Each CTL refinery will cost about as much as an aircraft carrier, and use about as much steel for its construction.

In addition, CONSOL Energy is planning a CTL plant in West Virginia, with startup slated for 2012. The goal is to annually produce 700,000 metric tons of methanol that can be used as feedstock for the chemical industry, as well as about 100 million gallons of liquid vehicle fuel (or about 7,000 barrels per day).[12] DKRW, founded by four former employees of Enron, is developing a liquefied coal plant near Medicine Bow, Wyoming, with a planned startup date of 2013. And American Clean Coal Fuels is investing $3.6 billion in a plant in Oakland, Illinois, with plans to produce 30,000 barrels of fuel per day and a startup in 2012 or 2013.[13]

Currently, while development of CTL enjoys bipartisan political support in the United States, European countries are slower to endorse the technology because of its climate implications.

Underground Coal Gasification

UCG offers an alternative to conventional coal mining for some resources that are otherwise not commercially viable to extract. The basic process consists of drilling one well into the coal to inject air or oxygen, and another to bring the resulting gas to surface. Then, underground combustion is initiated. Often the natural permeability of the coal is too low to allow the gas to pass through it, and various methods must be used to fracture the coal. A recent variation on the method involves drilling dedicated inseam boreholes and a moveable injection point, using technology adapted from the oil and gas industry.

Once the gas has been withdrawn, it can be purified and used to produce chemicals or liquid motor fuels, or to generate electricity.

In 1868, Sir William Siemens was the first to propose gasifying waste and unminable coal in place, without having first to extract it from mines.[14] An initial experiment along these lines began in County Durham (UK) in 1912; however, work was left incomplete at the commencement of World War I, and no further UCG efforts were undertaken in Western Europe until after World War II.

Meanwhile, however, the USSR began UCG research in the 1930s, leading to industrial-scale implementation in the 1950s and '60s at several coal sites. Soviet interest in the technology subsequently declined after the discovery of extensive and cheap natural gas resources; today only one site in Uzbekistan is still operational.

Renewed European interest in UCG emerged between the years 1944 and 1959 due to energy shortages. Research focused on gasification of coal in thin seams and at shallow depth. Although an attempt was made to develop a commercial pilot plant in Newman Spinney in the United Kingdom in 1958, all European UCG work stopped during the 1960s due to falling energy prices.

The United States started an experimental UCG program in 1972, building on Russian experience, and European interest was rekindled in 1989 when the European Working Group on UCG recommended a series of trials to evaluate commercial feasibility. The trials took place in Spain, the United Kingdom, and Belgium, with mixed results.

More recently, Australia conducted a trial lasting from 1999 to 2003, and has plans for a commercial startup in the immediate future; and China initiated several UCG trials, of which 16 are ongoing.

Some highly inflated claims have been made regarding the potential of this technology to turn a large proportion of coal resources into reserves. However, the reality is that UCG is only practical if coal seams possess special properties. They must be between 300 and 1,900 feet

(100 and 600 meters) underground (preferably more than 1,000 feet), with a seam thickness of more than 15 feet (5 meters). There must be minimal discontinuities in the seam, and no large water aquifers close by. The coal itself must have ash content less than 60 percent. Altogether, this description applies to only a small portion of the world's coal reserves. The World Energy Council estimates that UCG will increase economically recoverable reserves by only 600 million tons, adding to the current world total of 847,488 million tons of official booked reserves.[15]

Thus, while UCG projects are expanding and the technology is headed for wider deployment, it is unlikely to dramatically increase the amount of coal that can be extracted and used worldwide.

Carbon Capture and Storage

The world demands growing quantities of energy, and developing countries especially need cheap energy. At the same time, the world faces a climate Armageddon due in great part to the effects of burning our cheapest and most abundant fossil energy resource, coal. For many energy experts, there seems to be only one way out of this impasse: capture the carbon from coal and bury it, while continuing to benefit from coal's cheap, abundant energy.

For the coal industry, which is concerned that coal is being cast as the main climate villain, this is a way to make their product look ecologically acceptable. For mainstream environmental organizations, CCS offers a strategy to reduce climate impacts without having to call for painful reductions in coal consumption, and thus in all likelihood a reduction in both total energy use and economic growth — a politically untenable position. The IPCC is also supportive, suggesting that CCS could someday provide up to 55 percent of the emissions reduction needed to avoid the worst effects of global warming.[16]

With endorsement from both the coal industry and climate scientists, there is little wonder that CCS is being embraced by policy makers. Wealthier countries (the United States, Australia, Europe, Japan) are committed to advance the technology with public funds, with the hope that as CCS gets cheaper with frequent application, it will become affordable by poorer countries like India and China. In early 2008, the Group of Eight (G-8) energy ministers, meeting in Japan, called for the launch of 20 large-scale CCS demonstration projects globally by 2010.[17]

There are three different types of CCS technologies being developed: post-combustion, pre-combustion, and Oxy-fuel combustion.

In post-combustion, the CO_2 is removed after coal is burned in conventional power plants. The technology is well understood but expensive to deploy.

In pre-combustion, the coal is partially oxidized in a gasifier (see IGCC, above); then the resulting syngas, consisting of carbon monoxide (CO) and hydrogen (H_2), is transformed into carbon dioxide (CO_2) and H_2. The CO_2 can be captured relatively easily prior to the combustion of the H_2 — which itself can be used for industrial processes or to fuel transportation.

In Oxy-fuel combustion, coal is burned in oxygen instead of air. To limit flame temperatures to the levels of conventional combustion, cooled flue gas (consisting of CO_2 and water vapor) is re-circulated and injected into the combustion chamber. The water vapor is collected via condensation, leaving an almost pure stream of CO_2 to be collected, transported, and stored. This method results in the highest percentage of carbon being captured from the fuel; however, the initial step of separating oxygen from air requires considerable energy, and so final electricity costs from such a system are likely to be high. A different version of this method, called chemical looping combustion (CLC), is currently being researched. It uses metal oxide particles as an oxygen carrier; these react with coal to make CO_2 and water vapor before being circulated to a second stage where they react with air, producing heat and regenerated metal oxide particles.

After CO_2 is captured, it must be transported to suitable storage sites. This will almost certainly be accomplished via pipeline. There are already approximately 4,000 miles (5,800 km) of CO_2 pipelines in the United States; these are currently being used to carry carbon dioxide to oilfields where it is injected to force oil toward boreholes to maintain production levels when natural oilfield pressure wanes. However, the market for CO_2 is limited and is destined to shrink in coming decades as depletion gradually forces the oil industry into retirement. Moreover, in the meantime the burning of additional oil derived from CO_2 - enhanced recovery methods will offset much or all of the reduction in CO_2 emissions that is achieved at the power plant, so this method of storage will not help much with climate mitigation efforts.

If and when carbon is captured on a large scale, power producers will have to pay for both CO_2 transport and storage. Transport will require the construction of thousands of miles of pipelines, and storage will require drilling and other infrastructure investments.

The main forms of permanent storage for captured CO_2 currently under discussion include gaseous storage in various deep geological formations (including saline formations and exhausted gas fields), liquid storage in the ocean, and solid storage by reaction of CO_2 with metal oxides to produce stable carbonates.

Geological storage, also known as geo-sequestration, involves injecting carbon dioxide directly into oilfields, gasfields, saline formations, unminable coal seams, and saline-filled basalt formations. Several pilot programs are testing the long-term storage of CO_2 in non-oil producing geologic formations.

Unminable coal seams can be used to store CO_2, which adsorbs to the surface of coal; however, only coal beds with adequate permeability will work for this purpose. There is a potential side benefit: as CO_2 is absorbed, coal releases previously absorbed methane, which can be recovered and sold to offset a portion of the cost of the CO_2 storage (however, methane burned or released into the atmosphere means added carbon emissions).

Saline formations containing highly mineralized brines have been used for storage of chemical waste in a few cases. These have a large potential storage volume and are commonly found, so the distances over which CO_2 would have to be transported could be minimized. However, relatively little is known about these formations on an individual basis, so each would have to be explored and evaluated, adding to costs.

Ocean storage could be accomplished by "dissolution" — injecting carbon dioxide by ship or pipeline to depths of 1,000 meters or more, where it would subsequently dissolve; by "lake" deposition, where CO_2 would be deposited directly onto the sea floor at depths greater than 3,000 m, where carbon dioxide, being denser than water, would form a "lake" that presumably would remain stable for a long time; by conversion of CO_2 to bicarbonates (using limestone); or by storing the carbon dioxide in solid clathrates (also known as methane hydrates — ice crystals enclosing molecules of methane) already existing on the ocean floor. The environmental impacts of oceanic storage are likely to be negative (the oceans are already suffering from acidification as a result of elevated atmospheric CO_2 levels), but no experiments have been performed on a large enough scale to indicate just how bad those impacts would be.

Mineral storage is done by reacting naturally occurring magnesium- and calcium-containing minerals with CO_2 to form carbonates, producing stable materials. The raw materials are abundant. However, the process is slow under ambient temperatures and pressures; speeding up the process would require large energy inputs.

Will sequestered carbon dioxide leak back into the environment, and at what rate? The IPCC has assessed the risks, and concludes that for well-selected, -designed, and -managed geological storage sites, 99 percent of CO_2 would likely be retained for over 1,000 years. With ocean storage, CO_2 retention would depend on depth, with 30-85 percent retained after 500 years for depths of 1,000-3,000 meters. Mineral storage would not pose any leakage risks.[18] However, liability issues regarding leaked CO_2 are already being explored, with Texas leading the way, having passed a bill assuming state liability and asserting the doctrine of sovereign immunity (in effect, no carbon leakage lawsuit in Texas could ever be litigated).

The biggest problems with implementing CCS are the added cost for electricity production, the long lead time for widespread application of the technology, and the sheer scale of the undertaking.

Capturing and storing carbon will require up-front investment in new infrastructure (including pipelines), and it will also increase operating costs at power plants. These higher costs will inevitably be passed along via high electricity rates. The GAO predicts that electricity from pre-combustion clean coal plants will cost up to 78 percent more than electricity from conventional coal plants, not counting the potential cost of carbon emissions permits.[19] Adding CCS technology to existing plants (post-combustion) would be still more expensive.

This added financial cost conceals an arguably even more important energy cost from CCS: capturing, moving, and storing carbon dioxide will require energy, making the process of producing electricity from coal less energy-efficient, at the very same time that the energy content of coal being mined is declining. For example, the IPCC estimates that a power plant using mineral storage would need 60 to 180 percent more energy than a power plant without CCS; thus, if this storage strategy were adopted, consumption of coal would need to more than double (in all likelihood) in order for society to realize an equivalent energy benefit.

According to a December 2006 GAO report, "[the DOE] and industry have not demonstrated the technological feasibility of the long-term storage of carbon dioxide captured by a large-scale, coal-based power plant,"[20] and the DOE doesn't expect to have demonstrated the feasibility for at least a decade. While several CCS research sites are likely to be operating within a few years, widespread commercial application of the technology is not likely until 2035 at the earliest (in US Senate testimony, Dr. Mark Myers, head of the US Geological Survey, forecast that widespread use of CCS could be possible "in the 2045 timeframe"[21]).

By that time, United States and world coal production will be headed downhill (assuming the EWG analysis is correct). Thus, society will be burdened simultaneously with four new, interlinked costs and risks with regard to coal:

- the need for substantial investment in new CCS technology;
- higher coal prices and shortages due to depletion;
- higher electricity generating costs due to the use of IGCC and CCS; and
- lower electricity generation efficiencies due to the use of CCS, requiring more coal to produce an equivalent amount of electricity.

On top of these economic and energy concerns, there is the practical matter of the sheer scale of the enterprise being proposed. The amount of carbon dioxide that would have to be moved is staggering. Right now, the most ambitious efforts to stash carbon dioxide are handling the gas at amounts totaling little more than a million tons a year. To have a meaningful impact on the growth in emissions from coal burning, carbon dioxide disposal would have to expand a thousand-fold.

Total world annual carbon dioxide production from the consumption and flaring of fossil fuels amounted to 28.2 billion tons in 2005. Of this, about 40 percent or 11.4 billion metric tons came from the burning of coal.[22]

Leaving open the question of which carbon storage method is chosen (although assuming that mineral storage is ruled out for reasons of cost), and assuming that the CO_2 is liquefied and stored at a temperature of zero degrees C (32F) and a pressure of 200 atmospheres (2,940 pounds per square inch), the density of the liquid would be 1,050 kilograms per cubic meter. This is slightly higher than the density of water (1,000 kg per cubic meter). Thus, the volume of liquid carbon dioxide that would need to be buried every year would be equal to 11,400 billion kg divided by 1,050 kg per cubic meter, which is 10.9 billion cubic meters, or 10.9 cubic kilometers.

To put this in perspective: World annual coal production is over 5 billion metric tons, which equates to only about 4 cubic kilometers. World annual total ore mined in all mining operations is 17 billion tons.[23] World annual total earth moved (for mining and construction, etc.) is estimated at 30-35 billion tons.[24] Assuming the average density of the earth moved was 2,500 kg per cubic meter, this equates to 30 trillion kg divided by 2,500 kg per cubic meter, or 12 cubic kilometers (compared to 10.9 cubic kilometers of CO_2 from coal needing to be sequestered). Within the larger CCS discussion, this information is a useful supplement to calculations of dollars per ton or dollars per kilowatt-hour. According to a recent MIT study, "The Future of Coal," "If 60% of the CO_2 produced from US coal-based power generation were to be captured and compressed to a liquid for geologic sequestration, its volume would about equal the total US oil consumption of 20 million barrels per day."[25] The study also concluded that an enormous increase in investment in industrial-scale demonstration plants would be required now even to know in 10 or 15 years if the technology can work at a meaningful scale.

Vaclav Smil of the University of Manitoba, in a recent letter to *Nature*, notes that we would need to handle a volume of CO_2 twice as large as the world's crude oil flows just to sequester one-quarter of the carbon dioxide emitted in 2005 by large stationary sources.[26]

A close look at the daunting economic, technical, and infrastructural challenges to implementing CCS coal leads inevitably to the conclusion that coal can be cheap or "clean" (relatively speaking), but not both. And if coal is about to get much more expensive anyway due to depletion and transport issues, then most nations are likely to deem the added cost required to make coal "clean" to be one burden too many.

Conclusions

Given plenty of cheap available energy, technology can work wonders. It is understandable that our society has idolized technology, given the spectacular societal changes it has wrought in the past century. In the last 20 years alone, computers, cell phones, and a suite of other digital communications technologies have created industries and fortunes, altered our habits, and morphed our vocabulary. The evolution of computers has been subject to Moore's Law, according to which processor speed, memory capacity, and even the resolution of digital cameras are expected to double every two years.

It is tempting to extrapolate these rapid developments in communication technologies to the fields of transportation and energy production. But in these areas, technological change is slower and more expensive, and more obviously dependent on continued consumption of non-renewable resources such as oil, natural gas, coal, and iron ore.

Each of the coal technologies surveyed here holds promise for addressing one problem or another. None of them is a magic bullet that can overcome long-term production declines of either coal or other fossil fuels due to the depletion of high-grade resources; nor can any of them, even if successfully deployed, truly make coal environmentally benign. All are expensive in economic terms; only IGCC, with its greater efficiencies, avoids also imposing new energy costs on society.

Time will tell which if any of these technologies will be deployed on a large scale. Meanwhile, one truism remains: Investing in new coal technologies means increasing our societal dependence on coal, and therefore exacerbating our collective vulnerability to inevitable coal supply problems.

8

Three Scenarios

A s we have seen, the fate of the world's economy and Earth's climate depend largely on coal. Given other constraints upon energy, what will happen if current trends for coal consumption continue, and how might those trends be altered?

Before exploring those questions, perhaps it would be helpful to review the main conclusions from previous chapters:

1. Reports on world coal supplies are almost always framed in terms of reserves-to-production ratios ("we have 150 years' worth"), which have been shown repeatedly to be useless for accurate forecasting. Only recently have a few analysts attempted peaking forecasts for world coal, and those forecasts show a likely peak for world coal production before mid-century, possibly as soon as 2025.

2. China is relying almost entirely on coal to fuel rapid economic growth, which is its economic-political survival strategy. But coal production growth cannot be sustained for long. This will have dramatic impacts on China's economic and political stability, as well as global geopolitics.

3. The United States probably has much less producible coal than official estimates suggest, given recent evidence cited in the National Academy of Sciences report (2007),[1] and there has been a historically consistent bias on the part of official agencies toward over-estimation of reserves.

While there is no danger of running out soon, the quality of produced coal is declining, while the expense of transport is rising. That means coal supply bottlenecks and more expensive electricity. These factors should inform all decisions about new power plants.

4. The global market for coal is changing. It is the world's fastest-rising energy source by volume, with exporters poised to capitalize on rising demand in China and India. However, this trend is being countered by the next one:

5. The biggest constraint on expanding coal production in most countries is transportation — the lack of adequate rail networks and shipping ports, and problems with moving coal by truck. Coal transport problems can only increase in the years ahead as a result of rising liquid fuel prices. In effect, Peak Oil may hasten Peak Coal.

6. All of this has profound implications for the global climate. Due to coal supply constraints, the worst scenarios for carbon emissions will not be realized. But dire scenarios for climate impacts might be, due to the fact that the sensitivity of climate to carbon dioxide emissions has been underestimated. Climate change mitigation policies are still needed and if implemented will almost certainly have a constraining impact on coal consumption.

7. New coal technologies (coal-to-liquids, or CTL; Carbon Capture and Storage, or CCS; Integrated Gasification Combined Cycle power plants, or IGCC; and Underground Coal Gasification, or UCG) are critical to coal's future. All are problematic, in differing degrees and for differing reasons. Coal supply limits will inhibit the development of all but UCG. This latter technology could in principle increase reserves, but it cannot be implemented on a broad scale because special and unusual geological resource conditions are necessary.

Given these realities and trends, it is possible to identify three paradigmatic scenarios for the coming three decades. The exercise is intended as an aid for planning and decision-making; the point is not to predict specific events. An infinite number of scenarios could be constructed, but for present purposes it is helpful to minimize their number. Doing so requires making several assumptions.

First, regarding the timing of fossil fuel production peaks, we will assume that Energy Watch Group is correct regarding coal (global peak around 2025). The pattern of new discoveries for oil and gas is assumed to follow well-established declining trends. Technical improvements in fossil fuel extraction continue, but only succeed in marginally buttressing production rates. Consequently, world oil production peaks in 2010 and world natural gas production peaks in 2025, although regional shortages (especially in North America and Europe) appear sooner.

Technical improvements are also made in renewable energy technologies, but there is no overwhelming breakthrough that can be implemented universally within the thirty-year period.

The Stern Review on the Economics of Climate Change (a 700-page report released on October 30, 2006 by economist Lord Stern of Brentford for the British Government) and the IPCC Working Group 3 reports, which discuss the costs of mitigating climate change, have adopted a method that takes the cost of mitigating one unit of carbon and multiplies this by the amount of mitigation needed. This results in estimates of mitigation costs that range from a one percent gain in GDP to a five percent GDP cost over a 40-year period (for example, Stern states that "... climate change mitigation is technically and economically feasible with mid-century costs likely to be around 1% of GDP. ...").[2] This method has been criticized on the grounds that it ignores the difficulties and limits of scaling up nuclear or renewable energy sources.[3] Therefore, in all three of the present scenarios, effort has been made to factor in limits to renewable and nuclear energy sources, as well as the net energy likely to be derived from renewable and nuclear energy sources, CCS, and depleting fossil fuel sources.

Net energy is at least as important as total available energy in enabling economic activity. Energy must be invested in order to obtain more energy, regardless of the nature of the energy resource or the technology used, and society relies on the final net energy gained from energy-harvesting efforts to operate its manufacturing, distribution, and maintenance systems. If net energy produced is a large percentage of total energy produced, this means that a relatively small portion of societal effort must be dedicated to energy production, and therefore most of society's resources are available for other purposes. In a society where energy is acquired through agriculture — which yields a low and variable energy profit — most of the population must be involved in farming in order to provide enough energy to fund the maintenance of a small hierarchy of managers, merchants, soldiers, etc., that makes up the rest of the societal pyramid. In the early decades of the fossil fuel era, the quantity of both total and net energy liberated by efforts to mine and drill for these fuels was unprecedented, and it was this abundance of cheap energy that enabled the growth of industrialization, urbanization, and globalization during the past two centuries. It took only a trivial amount of effort in exploration and drilling to obtain an enormous energy return on energy invested (EROEI). But industry tended first to find and extract the coal, oil, and gas that were highest in quality and easiest to access; thus with every passing decade the net energy derived from fossil fuel extraction has declined. In the early days of the US oil industry, for example, a 100:1 net energy profit was common, while it is estimated that current US exploration efforts yield little more than a 1:1 energy payback.

In addition, alternatives to conventional fossil fuels generally have a much lower EROEI than coal, oil, or gas did in their respective heydays. For example, ethanol production from corn is estimated to have at best a 1.5:1 positive net energy balance;[4] it therefore is effectively useless as an energy source. Solar and wind do considerably better, with EROEI estimated in the range of 10-15:1[5] However, solar and wind are limited by their variability, which makes it impossible to replace fossil fuel-based generating capacity with either wind or solar generation capacity on a 1:1 basis.[6]

As the net energy available to society declines, increasing constraints will be felt on economic growth, and also on the adaptive strategies (which require new investment — example: the building of more public transport infrastructure) that society would otherwise deploy to deal with energy shortages. More of society's resources will have to be devoted directly to obtaining energy, and less will be available for all of the activities that energy makes possible. The immediately noticeable

Fig. 37

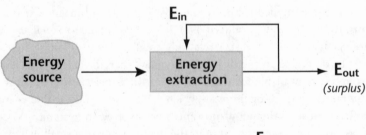

$$\text{Energy return on investment (EROI)} = \frac{E_{out}}{E_{in}}$$

Think of net energy in terms of the number of people in society engaged in energy production. If EROEI = 1, then everyone is involved in energy production and there is no one available to take care of society's other needs. If the EROEI is 100, then one person is involved in energy production and 99 are doing other things — building houses, teaching, taking care of the sick, cooking, selling real estate, etc. If we have two energy workers and 98 folks doing other things, then EROEI = 50; and similarly with four folks getting energy and 96 doing other things, EROEI = 25. With 8 getting energy and 92 doing other things (EROEI = 12.5) there may begin to be problems finding enough folks who are trained at getting energy while others build the tools and infrastructure for them to work (drilling rigs or tools for making solar panels). With 16 getting energy and 84 doing other things (EROEI = 6.25) serious problems

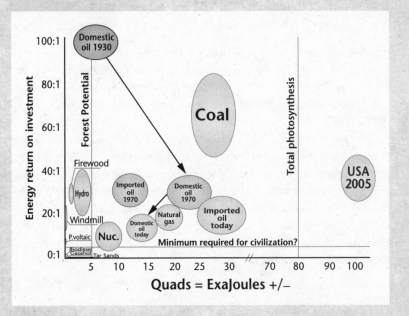

Fig. 38: *The relative EROEI and capacity of various energy sources. Modern industrial societies require energy sources high in both attributes (the upper right area of the chart). Unfortunately, most renewable sources of energy are limited in one or the other parameter, and thus occupy the lower left area of the chart.*

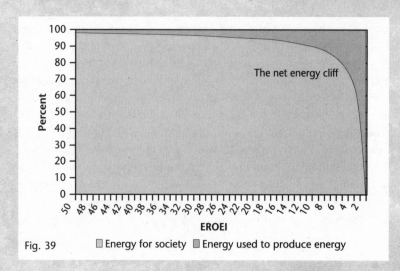

Fig. 39   ☐ Energy for society ☐ Energy used to produce energy

may become apparent, since 84 people may not be enough to provide for all of the needs of the 16, especially in view of the fact that half of the larger group may consist of children, the elderly, and disabled persons. With 16 energy workers and 42 others providing everything else, industrial society may not be viable.

Archaeologist Lynn White estimated that hunter-gatherer societies operated on a 10:1 net energy basis.[7] Since hunter-gatherer societies are the simplest human groups in terms of technology and degree of social organization, 10:1 should probably be regarded as the average minimum EROEI for the maintenance of human existence (though groups of humans could likely survive for occasional periods, up to a year or two in duration, of lower EROEI). Since industrial society entails much greater levels of complexity, its minimum EROEI must be substantially higher.[8]

symptoms will be rising costs of bare necessities and a reduction in job opportunities in fields not associated with basic production.

The scenarios that follow do not reflect potential political events such as wars, revolutions, or natural disasters. While such events are nearly certain to occur, they are impossible to forecast with regard to magnitude or timing.

The scenarios also do not attempt to forecast specific climate impacts resulting from burning coal, though Scenario 1 will entail far worse such impacts than will Scenarios 2 or 3.

Since we are removing such political and environmental eventualities (most or all of which would presumably make matters worse) from our calculus it would be wrong to regard any of the three scenarios as "worst-case."

In none of the scenarios does nuclear power become a dominant energy source. This is due to the high initial cost and long lead time of power plant construction, and also to geological limits on the availability of high-grade uranium ore. Breeder reactors or thorium reactors could theoretically solve the latter problem (at least temporarily), but breeders have not been a success and thorium reactors are still on the drawing boards. The world would require approximately 10,000 new one-gigawatt plants to provide all current energy needs, but there is an insufficiency of investment capital and trained workers to enable even a significant fraction of that number to be built within the 30-year horizon of these scenarios. Thus, while world nuclear capacity is indeed likely to grow over the period under discussion, it is highly unlikely to grow more quickly than is reflected here.

Other implicit assumptions as well as the explicit details of the scenarios are derived from the Post Carbon Institute's ongoing scenario planning discussions, which in turn are continually informed by models and calculations formulated by other organizations and analysts.

Scenario 1. Maximum Burn Rate

This is the default scenario, based on projecting existing consumption and depletion trends into the future, with no mitigating policies being implemented to change those trends significantly.

In this scenario, the world's industrialized and industrializing nations make every effort to maintain economic growth by conventional means — that is, by continually increasing consumption of energy and raw materials. They continue to burn greater amounts of coal in hopes that economic growth will enable an eventual transition to a more sustainable energy regime and perhaps a more equitable distribution of economic goods. Efforts to boost efficiency are driven solely by market mechanisms, such as higher oil prices.

By the end of the 30-year period, renewable sources of energy (excluding hydro power and the use of wood for heat) grow to provide five times their current contribution, or five percent of total world energy (this figure assumes a constant contribution from fossil fuel energy), requiring an investment of approximately ten trillion of today's dollars. Nuclear power doubles, requiring the investment of between three and nine trillion dollars (200 older power plants are retired during this period, while 600 equivalent-capacity new ones are constructed); in the end, nuclear provides a 12 percent share of total world energy (current share: three percent).[9]

As oil becomes increasingly scarce and costly, many nations (led by China and the United States) turn to CTL to provide synthetic liquid fuels, especially for military and air transport purposes, and to coal gasification to provide substitute feedstocks for chemicals and nitrogen fertilizer production. There is also a surge in the manufacture of electric automobiles, raising the requirement for electricity. All of these developments add to the already growing demand for coal, and exacerbate coal shortages and price increases.

The scenario unfolds through its 30-year timeframe on a decade-by-decade basis as follows:

2010 to 2020: With global oil production peaking in 2010, high petroleum prices drive all subsequent events. Impacts from quickly rising yet highly volatile oil prices ripple throughout the economic system, affecting the transportation and agricultural sectors most severely.

While increasing coal demand resulting from implementing CTL technology and from the proliferation of electric vehicles begins to be felt early in the decade, it is of relatively little consequence until after 2015, but then quickly becomes significant, putting substantial upward pressure on coal prices.

Rising demand for coal (and unstable supply) in China and India leads to a growing internationalization of the coal market. Even major coal producers with large reserves, such as the United States, find it difficult to maintain low domestic prices as export demand competes with domestic demand.

Rising transport costs (due to oil depletion) also work to increase coal prices, both internationally and domestically.

Meanwhile, high transport costs favor repatriation of manufacturing processes to North America and Europe, and work against the export-based economies of Asia. In effect, globalization goes into reverse.

Coal consumers are caught several ways at once: if more transport fuel is made from coal to lower transport costs, that means increased coal demand and higher prices; but if such efforts are not undertaken or are not successful, that also means higher coal prices (due to higher transport costs). If electric cars proliferate, that means more electricity demand, more coal demand, and hence higher prices.

Coal production in China peaks within this decade, leading to severe grid outages. The situation in India is likely to be even worse; coal supply problems were already apparent in 2008. Both economies are devastated by the resulting energy shortages, as well as by the dramatic fall of demand for export goods in the United States and Europe. Pakistan, Bangladesh, and Nepal, as well as some island nations and some African and Central American countries suffer worst of all: in these nations, societal collapse is possible within the decade due to energy shortages and high food prices.

The United States produces more coal and, at least during the early years of the decade, exports more to the coal-hungry economies of Asia. However, this only hastens America's domestic coal production peak.

While the US economy is somewhat buoyed by repatriation of manufacturing, much higher energy costs result in a drastic decline in material standards of living.

2020 to 2030: Coal becomes even more expensive and scarce as production declines in China and India, putting additional pressure on international export supplies.

Production in the United States levels off and, late in the decade, begins to slide. The energy content of produced coal continues to fall, while the effort and cost of production increase.

Other nations are in essentially the same predicament: not only is total coal production worldwide leveling off (and falling in most instances), but the net energy from coal production is clearly declining. In other words, at the risk of repeating myself, just as supplies are stagnating (and in China and India falling), the amount of coal needed in order to deliver a constant amount of useful energy to society is growing. Further, the amount of coal available for export is now declining rapidly as coal-producing nations use more of their output domestically.

At the same time, world oil and gas production are now falling sharply and available exports are down to less than half of 2010 levels, so only countries that produce oil domestically have any significant quantities to use for transportation, manufacturing, or heating. Thus, demand for the products of coal gasification and liquefaction grows rapidly.

By this time, all new automobiles are electric, although demand for new cars has fallen dramatically due to the contraction of the global economy. Telecommuting has been maximized, but has proven unreliable due to grid outages.

The passenger airline industry, airfreight, and military aircraft are running largely on CTL and perhaps some advanced forms of biofuels. However, flight traffic is only a small fraction of its former magnitude. Only the very wealthy travel by air, and delivery of goods is almost entirely by surface transport.

Severe, ongoing grid outages spread to the United States and Europe. This is due in part to the aging of grid infrastructure and prior failure to invest in upgrades; however, coal and natural gas supply problems also play an important role. The lack of reliable electricity supplies has a devastating impact on economic activity. The wealthy provide themselves with solar panels and diesel generators — but fuel for generators is hard to come by (this is yet another growing demand point for CTL). Computer networks begin to fail, including networks that transmit credit card, banking, and investment information. Public health, water treatment, and water delivery are also impacted.

Material living standards in the United States and Europe continue to plummet. Unemployment, homelessness, and hunger plague cities, suburbs, and rural regions alike. However, many less-industrialized nations fare even worse. Only the few nations that have domestic sources of oil, gas, or coal do relatively well, although the word "relatively" must be stressed, as lack of domestic manufacturing or food production capability is not easily made up for through trade with the rest of the world.

2030 to 2040: Coal is very costly indeed and little is being exported. Natural gas output is clearly in decline in almost all countries that produce it. The export trade in oil is virtually gone as nations that still produce oil are using nearly all of their output domestically.

The lack of prior investment in renewable energy generation and low-energy infrastructure (e.g., public transport systems) is sorely felt. However, energy shortages are so severe that such investments are in most cases no longer possible. The problem is not a lack of financial capital (large quantities of money can always be printed), but of energy. Whatever energy is available must be applied to urgent efforts to support basic services; there is little or none left over for the development, manufacturing, and transport of solar panels, wind turbines, or other renewable energy technologies.

Because of prior failure to invest in public transport, societies must make do with crumbling remnants of highways, though there is little or no fuel for cars or trucks. Tires (even bicycle tires) have become unaffordable or unavailable, and road repairs are nearly impossible due to shortages of asphalt.

While soaring energy prices are onerous to nearly every segment of society, shortages are worse. Without fuel or electrical power, the foundations of modern life crumble.

With truck fleets unable to move for lack of fuel and passable roads, both urban and rural areas experience rising mortality due to poor distribution of food and medicines. Lack of home heat in winter months also contributes to soaring death rates.

Farmers are unable to obtain seeds, fertilizers, and other needed inputs; they cannot operate tractors and other machinery; nor can food be processed or stored in quantity. Regional and seasonal famines begin to impact even formerly wealthy nations.

Grid failure becomes the norm; lights are on only occasionally and electricity is strictly rationed. Communication networks are drastically reduced in scope and are continually strained. Industrial activity contracts and gradually disappears.

Only those nations with high remaining levels of subsistence agriculture or residual domestic fossil fuel resources escape economic devastation.

For many nations, sometime during this decade, social order breaks down and centralized national government ceases to function.

Blackout.

Scenario 2. The "Clean" Solution

This second scenario is essentially the same as the first, with one pivotal difference: governments undertake coordinated efforts to mitigate the impacts of climate change through massive investments in technology to capture and store carbon emissions from the burning of coal. This effort entails massive investments in IGCC power plants.

The size of the investment made to implement IGCC and CCS is sufficient to preclude the simultaneous rollout of massive new nuclear or renewable energy generation infrastructure. Thus, as in Scenario 1, energy from nuclear power only doubles and energy from renewable sources (excluding hydro) increases only five-fold.

Only part of CCS investment comes directly from government; the rest flows from the electrical power industry, mandated by cap-and-trade mechanisms or carbon taxes.

The price of electricity rises much faster in this scenario than in the first. However, other developments are generally similar: fossil fuel depletion leads again to the collapse of economies that are unprepared for and vulnerable to supply contraction and rising costs, although coal depletion is somewhat slowed temporarily while societies go through the decade-long process of developing CCS technologies and infrastructures, since the scenario assumes that governments mandate that no new coal power plants be built except those that capture carbon. However, net energy declines even faster than in Scenario 1, with the energy costs of CCS being imposed on top of declining resource quality and depletion. The same problems appear in aviation, farming, and grid and road maintenance as described in the first scenario.

2010 to 2020: CCS is not yet ready for broad deployment, but political commitment to climate mitigation prevents expansion of conventional coal power without the new technology. This in effect forces a reduction in coal consumption, delaying the world coal production peak by a decade.

However, for a world reeling from petroleum shortages, a stagnation or decline of electricity supplied from coal only exacerbates the crisis. Load-shedding, brownouts, and blackouts become commonplace, even in wealthy nations. The price of electricity soars.

For China, the adoption of CCS represents a fateful choice. Assuming, for the sake of this scenario, that as of 2010 no new Chinese coal electricity generating capacity is built without CCS, this means at least a decade (the minimum lead time for development of the technology) in which power generation grows only through additions from renewables and nuclear. China's economy, already hard-hit by a shrinkage of Western demand for its exported manufactured goods as well as by liquid fuel scarcity, must now also contend with more frequent and longer domestic electricity outages.

Similarly dire consequences are forecast for India's economy during the first decade of Scenario 2: more frequent and lengthening electrical power interruptions impose severe limits on economic activity.

During this decade, all coal-consuming nations commit large investment sums toward the development of CCS demonstration sites. Research on carbon storage is undertaken on a region-by-region basis.

The development of CTL to supplement declining liquid fuels is delayed until carbon storage can be worked out.

Altogether, in Scenario 2 this decade is more economically challenging than in Scenario 1, and especially so for the Asian economies.

2020 to 2030: Deployment of CCS now begins. Large investments are made in building out IGCC/CCS power plants and in moving and storing CO_2.

The delay in implementing CCS technology has resulted in changes in the world's rate of coal production: while, during the 2010 to 2020 decade, production declined, it now begins to increase again. However, with CCS technology the amount of useful energy being derived from the burning of coal is lower, so net energy declines significantly even as energy production efforts increase.

Now that CO_2 storage sites have been worked out, CTL with CCS can be deployed. This helps somewhat to mitigate the rapidly worsening petroleum shortages. However, transport of coal is by now a serious problem, as conventional diesel fuel for trains and trucks is scarce and very expensive, and the amount of liquid fuel that can be produced from CTL is limited. Moreover, the net energy from CTL fuel production with CCS is very low indeed.

Altogether, even though this decade sees higher coal consumption, the energy problems of society worsen.

As in Scenario 1, the impacts are more serious for some nations than for others. Those that are better able to afford CCS are able to implement it on a larger scale faster, and can thus burn more coal.

2030 to 2040: By now CCS is being installed in all coal power plants. New IGCC facilities come on line in large numbers and older, conventional power plants are either retired or retrofitted. CTL with CCS is also still expanding, though its low net energy yield makes fuel production practical only for uses where liquids are essential (primarily for aircraft).

But coal shortages, which would have begun a decade earlier in Scenario 1, are now appearing as world coal production goes into decline.

As coal prices soar and shortages become widespread, and as oil and gas supply problems worsen, the total energy available to societies drops quickly.

A less obvious but even more severe challenge is the decline in net energy — which, again, is worse in this scenario than in Scenario 1 due to the added energy costs of CCS. An increasing proportion of available energy must be reinvested in energy production activities, leaving ever less for transportation, housing, health care, education, research, and all of the other functions of a healthy economy. Because societies have not planned for a reduction in net energy, this translates to massive unemployment, shortages of basic necessities, and system failures.

It is clear by this time that insufficient investment has been made in renewable energy sources and energy conservation. But, as in Scenario 1, it is too late to change course.

Grid failures becomes widespread; communication networks are strained; industrial activity contracts. In many nations, social order breaks down and centralized national government ceases to function.

Blackout.

Scenario 3. Post Carbon Transition

In this scenario maximum effort is directed toward transitioning entire societies to a sustainable (i.e., renewable) energy regime as quickly as possible.

Policy makers recognize early in the scenario period that a planned, coordinated reduction in energy consumption throughout society will be necessary to achieve this goal, because even with maximum effort it will be impossible to increase energy supplies from renewable sources quickly enough to offset fossil fuel limitations.

Not only will proactive reductions in total energy consumption be required, but also a deliberate (rather than ad hoc or reactive) adjustment to a lower net-energy societal regime. This will entail shifting employment and investment back toward basic productive activities. In poor nations, it will mean developing policies that support subsistence agriculture rather than urbanization.

All of this in turn will require a new economic paradigm based on the "steady-state" economic theories pioneered by ecological economist Herman Daly.[10] Rather than promoting ever-higher levels of consumption as the goal of economic development and promising to create conditions in which individual consumption will increase, government must commit itself to making life better in other ways. This will require measuring economic growth in terms of human welfare (education,

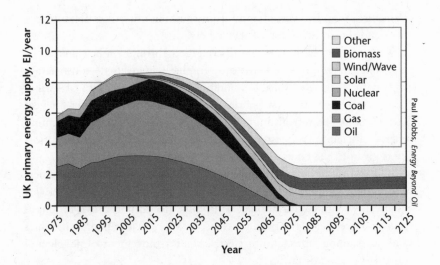

Fig. 40: *This chart reflects one analyst's attempt to chart an energy transition for the United Kingdom. His assumptions about the future availability of oil, gas, and coal are likely optimistic. Nevertheless, the general trajectory of the energy future outlined here — from a period of growth in energy from fossil fuels to one of decline in those energy sources accompanied by the rapid development of renewables, leading to a steady-state condition in the future — conforms well with Scenario 3 as discussed in the text.*

health, cultural expression) and environmental stability rather than GDP and material throughput.

Both to avert the inevitable effects of coal depletion and also to reduce climate impacts, the decision is made to phase out coal as quickly as possible — a reduction of five percent per year. This has implications primarily for electricity generation and steel production.

Since investments are required for updating power grids in any case, it is decided to develop a system of distributed power generation in order to maximize the ease of input from local renewable sources. At the same time, some new long-distance transmission lines are needed to bring electricity from places where renewable sources are abundant to coastal cities where the demand is greatest.

In this scenario, electricity is rationed earlier rather than later in order to aid the process of adaptation to a lower-energy regime.

Steel is rationed to industrial users by quota so as to be reserved primarily for transition efforts such as the production of rails for public transport. Steel is diverted away from the building of private automobiles and the construction of skyscrapers.

Cement production is also discouraged through policy due to its high energy requirements. Instead, emphasis is given to construction with natural, locally available building materials, the design of smaller passive solar structures (six stories or fewer) clumped together for heat savings, and the retrofitting of existing building stock for maximum energy efficiency. Only essential roads are maintained; otherwise, priority is given to the construction of rail networks.

Oil and gas are likewise rationed, with petroleum reserved for emergency vehicles, public transport vehicles, and necessary air travel (for political, scientific, educational, and public health purposes). Emphasis is given to reducing the need for transportation by localizing economies and redesigning cities, and to electric rail for movement of people and goods over long distances.

The government not only funds research and development of renewable energy, which grows to 25 times current capacity, but also creates incentives (such as feed-in tariffs) that encourage large-scale private investment. Altogether, a minimum of ten percent of GDP is annually devoted to the renewable energy transition during this 30-year period.

National energy departments and ministries undertake the task of analyzing the various alternative energy sources available, ranking them regionally for EROEI, scalability, environmental impacts, and other essential criteria. This gives localities a sound basis for directing public and private investment.

Nuclear power is phased out during the 30-year scenario period through attrition of older power plants and the decision not to replace them. This is done in view of limits to uranium supplies, the difficulties likely to be encountered by a lower-energy society in managing and safeguarding nuclear waste, and the need to reduce cement and steel production and consumption.

Since policy makers are now concerned more with the long-term sustainability of human society than with short-term competitive advantages among and between nations, more attention is paid to consumption patterns of renewable natural resources such as fresh water (from aquifers or glaciers), topsoil, oceans, and forests. This concern imposes further limits on conventional economic growth. Efforts are also directed toward the formulation of humane but ecologically sound population policies, with the understanding that if per capita consumption falls but population continues to grow, gains in sustainability will be wiped out.

National and local governments encourage young people to take up small-scale agriculture through low-interest loans; land reform; subsidized education; support for local, integrated food systems; and a withdrawal of support for agribusiness cartels. Government also supports the creation of career opportunities in natural building; energy efficiency retrofitting, monitoring, and consulting; and installation of renewable energy infrastructure.

Europe (excluding the United Kingdom) and Japan are perhaps best poised to afford the transition to renewable energy. The United States will be handicapped by its poor rail system, its high dependence on cars and trucks, and its highly industrialized food system. Russia and other major fossil fuel producers will need to use all of the income from diminishing production of oil, gas, and coal to fund the transition. China and India will have greater difficulty in the early period of transition because their current coal-based economic development model is taking them in the wrong direction fast. Poor, less-industrialized nations will leapfrog the fossil fuel-based development model (which is quickly becoming unaffordable in any case) and will prioritize traditional subsistence agriculture supplemented by the lowest-cost versions of renewable electricity generation technologies.

2010 to 2020: As world oil production peaks, society experiences an economic shock, manifesting as a global economic depression, accompanied by unemployment, bank failures, and homelessness. However, policy makers understand the causal role of the inevitable depletion of fossil fuels and recognize that a systemic and fundamental shift in governmental philosophy and policy is required. Rather than focusing just on finding short-term fixes for the symptoms of economic collapse, they undertake to plan for a long-term redesign of industrial society, using widespread societal distress and calls for relief as political leverage for this larger project.

Reorganization on this scale cannot successfully be imposed from the top down. On the other hand, efforts from grassroots volunteer organizations will fail unless supported by policy makers. Thus from the outset, the transition is designed to support community organizing via relocalization groups while providing investment and regulation to guide the transformation of large-scale societal infrastructure.

This period could perhaps be described as the transition to the transition. Society is mobilized around the great task of moving away from dependence on fossil fuels, a project that will reshape every nation and every industry, and alter the daily experience of virtually everyone on the planet.

The investment of at least 10 percent of GDP annually on the energy transition entails the availability of less money for other purposes — including household spending and the maintenance of military budgets. Governments are able to mobilize such a transformation of spending priorities only by engaging the entire polity in the project (so that only the details of the transition are subjects for political dispute, not the transition *per se*). In addition, the primary financial stakeholders in society — including weapons manufacturers, banks, and fossil fuel companies — are engaged in the transition rather than marginalized, as otherwise they would likely derail the effort.

The continued financing of existing debts, given much lower levels of disposable income, challenges the entire economic-financial system, necessitating fundamental monetary reforms and the shift to a steady-state economic paradigm.

In the early years of transition, revenues to fund renewables and efficiency could be obtained through higher taxes on the consumption of fossil fuels (this would also, of course, help reduce the use of those fuels). However, as fossil fuels deplete and decline, this would entail a declining revenue stream, so this is not chosen as a primary funding stream for the transition.

Banks are required to offer preferred lending rates for renewable energy and energy efficiency projects, while feed-in tariffs guarantee profits from investments in the transition.

As some industries are de-emphasized (fossil fuel production, automobiles, road building, large-scale construction projects), government at all levels offers support for workers to learn new skills.

Altogether, this shift of spending priorities, with its attendant political, economic, monetary, and financial components, must be planned and implemented during this first decade of the scenario period as a necessary basis for all that is to follow.

In most cases, investments in alternatives appear to yield poor returns at first, as available energy declines even as societal effort gains strength and focus. There are a few bright spots, however: newer electric motors, twice as efficient as many older ones still in use, save large amounts of energy throughout the economy. And coordinated, purposeful effort on the part of society as a whole results in a widespread sense of engagement and psychological satisfaction.

Policies to control population sizes must begin early in the scenario period in order to be effective.

Likewise, international agreements on sharing resources and technology must be implemented early if conflicts are to be avoided, as some nations are better prepared than others to undertake the transition, while a few are already at a critical juncture regarding availability of water, food, and fuel.

In sum, the redirection of resources that characterize this initial decade of energy transition can be compared to the wartime mobilization that occurred in the United States in 1942, when the production and sale of cars and trucks for private use were banned, driving for pleasure was outlawed, and residential and highway construction was halted, with policy effectively directing every part of the economy's output to the war effort (this wholesale switch of production to military equipment resulted in the greatest expansion of industrial output in America's history). A similar level of focus and productivity — coordinating government, industry, education, entertainment, and media messaging — will be required in order to achieve a renewable energy economy.

2020 to 2030: This constitutes the main phase of the transition: investment streams are in place and the retraining and re-skilling of the populace have been largely accomplished; now is when the actual work is done. Enormous numbers of renewable energy installations are built. Millions of homes and public buildings are retrofitted. Cities are redesigned. Public transit systems and inter-city rail networks are constructed. Small low-input farms take root throughout the countryside.

The ongoing localization of economic activity yields benefits in jobs and careers within communities, and a sense of participation in social, economic, and political processes. People can see what they and their neighbors are accomplishing.

Worldwide, the primary demographic trend begins to shift from urbanization to ruralization. Farms are providing not only food, but also energy and raw materials, and more farmers — both in raw numbers and as a percentage of society — are needed in order to accomplish this.

Total energy and net energy continue to decline. However, government now measures growth with social welfare indicators that are starting to show improvement.

2030 to 2040: During this decade, as a result of efforts in the previous 20 years, both the amount of total energy and the proportion of net energy available to society finally stabilize. World population also stabilizes and begins to decline toward a long-range target of two billion — which, when achieved, will enable per-capita levels of consumption above the poverty level for the entire human family. Human society is on the road to sustainability.

Relative international stability has also been achieved, with a reduced level of economic inequity between nations. Nations that have transitioned first and fastest are best off, while those with high populations — especially urban populations — relative to carrying capacity (measured by per capita availability of water and arable land, and by assessment of intact ecological systems) are worse off, but the gap is being narrowed through the sharing of renewable energy technologies.

International trade continues at a substantially reduced level, almost entirely by way of water and rail, with most trade focusing on technology rather than the transport of ores, fuels, and grains.

Agriculture has become smaller-scale, with hundreds of millions of gardeners practicing nutrient recycling within a low-input, high-yield, localized, diversified regime.

History is not at an end: nations, businesses, and individuals still seek competitive advantage, culture still evolves through individual and societal artistic achievements, and economies still shift as the result of technical discoveries and inventions as well as the evolution of ecological systems. But humankind has entered a new era of collective awareness of environmental limits.

Comparing the Options

Many readers may find all three scenarios unpalatable, preferring instead to envision a future characterized by continually increasing rates of extraction, production, and consumption. However, the eventual end of growth in this sense is inevitable within a finite world, and overwhelming evidence suggests that such limits to growth will appear by mid-century one way or another. The three scenarios above were chosen because they depict the primary pathways whereby societal engagement with those limits seems most likely to occur.

The first scenario would have the worst environmental consequences of the three. While the impacts of climate change have not been factored into any of the scenarios, it is safe to assume that, by the end of the scenario period, epic droughts and storms would be exacerbating an already miserable situation in the case of Scenario 1.

The second scenario has better environmental consequences than the first; however, it has the worst economic profile of the three: worse than Scenario 1 in the first two decades, much worse than Scenario 3 in the third. Despite this, it is the scenario most often advocated by policy makers and the fossil fuel industry, because it appears to preserve economic growth (through continued coal consumption) while simultaneously achieving climate protection. However, the conventional formulation of this scenario does not take resource depletion or net energy decline into account. Doing so yields societal consequences that are about the same as, or perhaps worse than, those for Scenario 1.

The third scenario has the best environmental profile of the three from a long-term perspective. It is also the only one of the three to avert economic and societal collapse. However, this outcome is achieved only by doing things that will be politically difficult, to say the least — fundamentally redesigning the world economic system while forging global resource, technology-sharing, and population agreements.

Because the second scenario leads to essentially same result as the first from an economic point of view, the three scenarios could be considered, in effect, to be only two — one that continues to rely on depleting fossil fuels (with or without carbon capture), and one in which those fuels are deliberately phased out.

In scenario exercises it is possible to outline coherent societal strategies and pathways, but reality is rarely so tidy. It is likely that some nations will hew to a Scenario 1 pathway while others pursue a Scenario 2 path, and still others a Scenario 3 path. Even within a single economy, there may be a mixture of strategies. For the United States, for example, it is easy to imagine a future similar to Scenario 1, but one with more investment in renewable energy, nuclear power, and energy efficiency; in this mixed scenario, even though a full conversion of coal electricity generation to CCS would be cost prohibitive, a partial conversion might avert some climate impacts. In that case the result might not be a relatively quick Blackout, but a slow fade to a dark shade of brownish gray — a persistence of industrial activity and organized society, but on a smaller scale and in a context of general environmental ruin and human suffering. This may in fact be the most likely route for

America, with other nations adopting differing scenario mixtures and experiencing somewhat differing versions of brownout fading to black.

However, if path 1 or 2 is chosen, a successful switch to the third later on will be difficult and largely ineffective due to a limit on the time available for transitioning (this adaptive time limit is imposed by resource depletion and declining resource quality). In order for the world to fully achieve the end result described for Scenario 3, efforts would have to begin immediately, and be broad in scale, with few nations (if any) refusing to participate.

As discussed in Chapter 6, we humans tend to discount the future. Thus, we favor the promise of an immediate benefit over a potentially greater one in the future, just as we tend to expend more effort to avoid an immediate threat than a greater one that may appear later. This tendency works in favor of Scenario 1, making it the path most likely actually to be followed (given that Scenario 2 entails more economic pain in the first decade, and Scenario 3 assumes deliberate reduction in fossil energy production and consumption together with an enormous and coherent societal effort that does not pay obvious dividends for 15 years or more).

However, this calculus could change. As actual oil shortages and coal price increases bite, policy makers may be forced to rethink strategies and consider paths that are currently unacceptable. For a Scenario 3 path to be adopted, policy makers would need to seize the moment, as Franklin Delano Roosevelt did in early 1942. High fossil fuel prices by themselves are more likely to encourage false and short-term solutions (corn-to-ethanol, more drilling for oil, or more coal production), but actual energy shortages could motivate fundamental change if leaders are poised to articulate and facilitate the way forward.

Final Words

The subtitle of this book makes reference to "the last energy crisis." Humanity has survived many previous energy crises, from the Pleistocene megafaunal extinctions up to the oil shocks of the 1970s. How could coal depletion amount to humanity's *final* energy problem?

If, as our scenario exercise suggests, there are really only two basic paths ahead — on one hand, the attempt to maintain maximum economic growth using fossil fuels of declining quality (with or without carbon capture and storage); or on the other, a scaling back of consumption, population, and economic growth so that all needs can be provided from renewable energy sources — then the end of coal means the last energy crisis in either a negative or a positive sense.

In the negative sense: Once world coal production peaks, unless nations are already well on the way toward a renewable energy economy, they won't have a high net energy source available to keep the lights on *and* fund a further transition that only begins at that time. The peak of world oil production in 2010 will impact the world economy profoundly. Without a coherent effort to proactively reduce energy consumption further while developing renewable sources, the decline of energy from coal toward the middle of the century will deliver a *coup de grace* to industrial civilization, making the maintenance of electrical grids problematic to impossible. We will then have come to the end of the road, having used nature's endowment of cheap, energy-dense fuels without having built a bridge to the future. What follows is the final Blackout.

If we do develop a renewable energy infrastructure and a steady-state economy based on a recognition of ecological limits, the period of coal's decline will constitute the last energy crisis in a positive sense: once we have adopted a no-growth economic paradigm and are relying on resources that are continually replenished, we may never again have to worry about energy supplies.

The choice before us could hardly be starker. Yet it is largely concealed by political rhetoric that is, at its core, unconsciously motivated by the future-discounting tendencies of human nature.

Coal enabled the beginning of the Industrial Revolution — the last two centuries of rapid growth in population, consumption, invention, manufacturing, and trade, whose fruits we now enjoy — and one way or another our policies toward coal will shape the end of this unique moment in human history. This could be, as Bill McKibben has written, the "End of Nature,"[11] and also the end of organized human life. Or it could be the pivotal moment when our species adapts to the fact that its planet's limits have been reached; and when it adopts policies, behaviors, and goals that enable it to inhabit this planet in a stable yet culturally satisfying fashion.

Fossil fuels have given us an amazing ride. But their gifts were delivered during one historically brief interval of ever-expanding consumption, when the global environment provided plenty of space for the dumping of industrial wastes (including CO_2), when population was low relative to the expanding (though temporary) carrying capacity opened up by fertilizers and irrigation, and when new inventions and discoveries came easily because energy was cheap and abundant.

Now we are moving into a different era characterized by the effects of resource depletion, by relentlessly falling net energy, and by the disappearance of environmental space in which wastes can be dumped without obvious and unacceptable consequences to human society. We have embarked on a century that will be defined by ecological limits, and by our response to those limits.

The temptation will be to apply the attitudes that seemed justifiable and profitable during the last century to the crises facing us in this one. The result, if we give in to that temptation, will be monumentally, historically, and conclusively catastrophic. Nowhere does this conclusion come with greater clarity than with regard to our national and global policies regarding coal. Quite simply: if we burn it, we cook the planet and ourselves, while losing out on the very economic benefits we are chasing.

We have only one narrow timeframe of opportunity for ensuring a desirable future for our species by reducing fossil fuel consumption while developing renewable energy sources and a sustainable economic paradigm.

The clock is ticking.

Notes

INTRODUCTION

1. International Monetary Fund, *Regional Economic Outlook: Sub-Saharan Africa* (Washington, DC: International Monetary Fund, May 2005), imf.org/external/pubs/ft/AFR/REO/2005/eng/01/pdf/ssareo.pdf.
2. David Robertson, Angela Jameson and Sam Coates, "Breakdowns Spark National Grid Crisis in Power Supply," *Times Online* (September 5, 2008), business. timesonline. co.uk/tol/business/industry_sectors/utilities/article4678321.ece.
3. Winston S. Churchill, *The World Crisis, 1911-1918*, vol. 1 (Free Press, 2005).
4. John Gever, Robert Kaufmann, David Skole and Charles Vorosmarty, *Beyond Oil: The Threat to Food and Fuel in the Coming Decades* (Cambridge, MA: Ballinger, 1987), 87.
5. Richard Heinberg, *The Oil Depletion Protocol: A Plan to Avert Oil Wars, Terrorism, and Economic Collapse* (Gabriola Island, BC: New Society, 2006).
6. Central Intelligence Agency, *The World Factbook*, cia.gov/library/ publications/the-world-factbook/docs/rankorderguide.html.
7. David Stradling and Peter Thorsheim, "The Smoke of Great Cities: British and American Efforts to Control Air Pollution, 1860-1914," *BNet* (January 1999), findarticles.com/p/articles/mi_qa3854/is_199901/ ai_n8833707/pg_1.
8. James B. Rice and Jill A. Janocha, "Coal Mining Injuries, Illnesses, and Fatalities in 2006," *Bureau of Labor Statistics* (June 27, 2008), bls.gov/opub/cwc/sh20080623ar01p1.htm.
9. Some sense of the human and environmental consequences of "mountaintop removal" can be gained by perusing the website "Appalachian Voices," appvoices.org/index.php?/site/mtr_overview/.
10. Robert J. Saiget, "China's Coal Addiction Causing Environmental Disaster," *Terra Daily* (November 6, 2006), terradaily.com/reports/China_Coal_ Addiction_Causing_Environmental_Disaster_999.html.

11. OECD/International Energy Agency, *China's Power Sector Reforms: Where to Next?* (Paris: Organisation for Economic Co-operation and Development, 2006), 13, iea.org/textbase/nppdf/free/2006/chinapower.pdf.

12. National Snow and Ice Data Center, "Sea Ice Conditions at the Annual Minimum on September 16, 2007," nsidc.org/news/press/2007_seaiceminimum/20070810_index.html.

13. "Is the Ocean Carbon Sink Sinking?" RealClimate, article posted November 1, 2007, realclimate.org/index.php/archives/2007/11/is-the-ocean-carbon-sink-sinking/.

14. John Vidal, "Global Food Crisis Looms as Climate Change and Fuel Shortages Bite," *The Guardian* (November 3, 2007), guardian.co.uk/environment/2007/nov/03/food.climatechange.

CHAPTER ONE

1. Edward Hull, *The Coal-Fields of Great Britain: Their History, Structure and Resources* (London: H. Rees, 1905); Hull, E, 1864. *The Geology of The Country Around Oldham, Including Manchester and its Suburbs (Memoir of the Geological Survey of Great Britain)*, Sheet 88SW.

2. Cutler Cleveland and Robert Costanza, "Energy Return on Investment (EROI)," *The Encyclopedia of Earth* (April 2008), eoearth.org/article/Energy_return_ on_investment_(EROI).

3. Energy Information Administration, *International Energy Outlook 2008* (Official Energy Statistics from the US Government, Report # DOE/EIA-0484, June 2008), Chapter 4, "Coal," eia.doe.gov/oiaf/ieo/coal.html. R/P ratios provided in Table 9, "World Recoverable Coal Reserves as of January 1, 2006," eia.doe.gov/oiaf/ieo/pdf/table9.pdf.

4. World Coal Institute, "Coal Transportation," worldcoal.org/pages/content/index.asp?PageID=93.

5. A coal-mining engineer in South Africa once described to me in conversation how cost-driven mining techniques often disregard poorer-quality resources, and do so in such a way that once an underground mine is shut down, it is likely never to be re-opened. Eugene N. Cameron's *At the Crossroads: The Mineral Problems of the United States* (John Wiley & Sons, 1986) discusses how "workings deteriorate, and cave-ins may occur" in abandoned mines, frequently leading to a situation where "costs of rehabilitation may become prohibitive," "mining of the poorer seams may never be resumed," and "the coal involved in such mines becomes a lost resource."

6. Eugene N. Cameron, *At the Crossroads: The Mineral Problems of the United States* (John Wiley & Sons, 1986), 43-45.

7. Gordon H. Wood, Jr., Thomas M. Kehn, M. Devereux Carter, and William C. Culbertson, "Coal Resource Classification System of the US Geological Survey," *Geological Survey Circular 891*, USGS, pubs.usgs.gov/circ/c891/.

8. David Strahan, "Coal: Bleak Outlook for the Black Stuff," *New Scientist*, 2639 (2008), environment.newscientist.com/channel/earth/mg19726391.800-coal-bleak-outlook-for-the-black-stuff.html.

9. Werner Zittel and Jörg Schindler, "Coal: Resources and Future Production," *EWG-Series No. 1/2007*, Energy Watch Group, (2007),

energywatchgroup.org/fileadmin/global/pdf/EWG_Report_Coal_
10-07-2007ms.pdf.

10. Mikael Höök, Werner Zittel, Jörg Schindler, and Kjell Aleklett, "A Supply-Driven Forecast for the Future Global Coal Production," contribution to ASPO (2008): 36, tsl.uu.se/UHDSG/Publications/Coalarticle.pdf.

11. Ibid., 37.

12. B. Kavalov and S.D. Peteves, *The Future of Coal* (Luxembourg: European Commission, Directorate-General Joint Research Centre, Institute for Energy, 2007), 4, ie.jrc.ec.europa.eu/publications/scientific_publications/2007/EUR22744EN.pdf.

13. Ibid., 36-38.

14. David B. Rutledge, "Hubbert's Peak, the Coal Question, and Climate Change," California Institute of Technology, presentation (2007), rutledge.caltech.edu/.

15. Jean Laherrère, "Peak (or Plateau) of Fossil Fuels," (paper presented at Energy, Greenhouse Gases and Environment, Universidade Fernando Pessoa, Porto, Portugal, 6-8 October 2008), aspofrance.viabloga.com/files/JL_Porto_long_2008.pdf.

16. M. King Hubbert, *Techniques of Prediction as Applied to the Production of Oil and Gas, in Oil and Gas Supply Modeling*, National Bureau of Standards Special Publication 631, ed. Saul I. Gass, (Washington: National Bureau of Standards, 1982), 16-141, rutledge.caltech.edu/King%20Hubbert%20Techniques%20of%20Prediction%20as%20applied%20to%20the%20production%20of%20oil%20and%20gas.pdf.

17. Kenneth Deffeyes, *Beyond Oil: The View from Hubbert's Peak* (New York: Hill and Wang, 2005).

18. World Energy Council, *2004 Survey of Energy Resources*, 20th edition, (London: World Energy Council, 2004), 9, worldenergy.org/documents/ser2004.pdf.

19. Jean Laherrère, e-mail message to author, April 17, 2008.

20. Thomas Thielemann, Sandro Schmidt, and J. Peter Gerling, "Lignite and Hard Coal: Energy Suppliers for World Needs until the Year 2100 — An Outlook," *The International Journal of Coal Geology* 72 (Issue 1, September 2007): 1-14, sciencedirect.com/science?_ob=ArticleURL&_udi=B6V8C-4NJWNJP-2&_user=6682544&_rdoc=1&_fmt=&_orig=search&_sort=d&view=c&_acct=C000050221&_version=1&_urlVersion=0&_userid=6682544&md5=e433f606890f77057a515cdf0330af4d.

CHAPTER 2

1. Robert C. Milici, "Production Trends of Major US Coal-Producing Regions," (in Proceedings of the International Pittsburgh Coal Conference, Pittsburgh, 1996), byronwine.com/files/coal.pdf.

2. Marius R. Campbell, "The Value of Coal-Mine Sampling," *Economic Geology*, vol. 2, no. 1, (1907): 48-57.

3. Andrew B. Crichton, "How Much Coal Do We Really Have? The Need for an Up-to-date Survey," *Coal Technology*, August 1948.

4. Palmer Putnam, *Energy in the Future* (New York: Van Nostrand, 1953).

5. Paul Averitt, *Coal Resources of the United States* (US Geological Survey Bulletin 1412, 1975), 131.

6. US Geological Survey, *National Coal Resource Assessment (NCRA)*, energy.cr.usgs.gov/coal/coal_assessments/summary.html.

7. Energy Information Administration, *Recoverable Coal Reserves at Producing Mines, Estimated Recoverable Reserves, and Demonstrated Reserve Base by Mining Method* (EIA, Report DOE/EIA 0584 (2007), Report Released: September 2008), eia.doe.gov/cneaf/coal/page/acr/table15.html.

8. Committee on Coal Research, Technology, and Resource Assessments to Inform Energy Policy, *Coal: Research and Development to Support National Energy Policy* (Washington, DC: The National Academies Press, 2007), 44, books.nap.edu/catalog.php?record_id=11977.

9. Ibid., 49.

10. Timothy J. Rohrbacher, Dale D. Teeters, Gerald L. Sullivan, and Lee M. Osmonson, *Coal Reserves of the Matewan Quadrangle, Kentucky — A Coal Recoverability Study* (USGS, US Bureau of Mines Circular 9355), pubs.usgs.gov/usbmic/ic-9355/.

11. Committee on Coal Research, Technology, and Resource Assessments to Inform Energy Policy, *Coal: Research and Development to Support National Energy Policy* (Washington, DC: The National Academies Press, 2007), 53, books.nap.edu/catalog.php?record_id=11977.

12. Werner Zittel and Jörg Schindler, "Coal: Resources and Future Production," *EWG-Series No. 1/2007,* Energy Watch Group, (2007): 30-39, energywatch-group.org/fileadmin/global/pdf/EWG_Report_Coal_10-07-2007ms.pdf.

13. B. Kavalov and S.D. Peteves, *The Future of Coal* (Luxembourg: European Commission, Directorate-General Joint Research Centre, Institute for Energy, 2007), 33-34, ie.jrc.ec.europa.eu/publications/scientific_publications/2007.php.

14. Thomas Thielemann, Sandro Schmidt, and J. Peter Gerling, "Lignite and Hard Coal: Energy Suppliers for World Needs until the Year 2100 — An Outlook," *The International Journal of Coal Geology* 72 (Issue 1, September 2007), sciencedirect.com/science?_ob=ArticleURL&_udi=B6V8C-4NJWNJP-2&_user=6682544&_rdoc=1&_fmt=&_orig=search&_sort=d&view=c&_acct=C000050221&_version=1&_urlVersion=0&_userid=6682544&md5=e433f606890f77057a515cdf0330af4d.

15. Mikael Höök, Werner Zittel, Jörg Schindler, and Kjell Aleklett, "A Supply-Driven Forecast for the Future Global Coal Production," contribution to ASPO (2008): 22, tsl.uu.se/UHDSG/Publications/Coalarticle.pdf.

16. David B. Rutledge, "Hubbert's Peak, the Coal Question, and Climate Change," California Institute of Technology, presentation (2007), rutledge.caltech.edu.

17. Jean Laherrère, "Combustibles Fossiles: Quel Avenir pour Quel Monde?" *Association pour l'étude des pics de production de pétrole et de gaz natural,* aspofrance.viabloga.com/files/JL-Versailles-long.pdf.

CHAPTER 3

1. Jerry C. Tien, "China's Two Major Modern Coal Projects," *Engineering and Mining Journal* (May 1, 1998).

2. According to the 1992 BP proven reserves estimate, borrowed from WEC data, 13.5 percent of China's coal reserves consist of lignite, 24 percent non-coking

bituminous coal, 28 percent coking bituminous coal, and 18.5 percent anthracite.

3. Tim Wright, "Growth of the Modern Chinese Coal Industry: An Analysis of Supply and Demand, 1896-1936," *Modern China* 7 (1981): 317-350, mcx.sagepub.com/cgi/reprint/7/3/317.

4. In 1987, the BP "Statistical Review of World Energy" listed reserves of 156.4 billion tons. In 1990, BP reported Chinese coal reserves as 152.8 billion tons. By 1992, the amount had fallen to 114.5 billion tons. Oddly, that official number has not changed in the succeeding 16 years, during which the nation has produced over 20 billion tons of coal.

5. Werner Zittel and Jörg Schindler, "Coal: Resources and Future Production," *EWG-Series No. 1/2007,* Energy Watch Group, (2007): 27, energywatchgroup.org/fileadmin/global/pdf/EWG_Report_Coal_. 10-07-2007ms.pdf.

6. B. Kavalov and S.D. Peteves, *The Future of Coal* (Luxembourg: European Commission, Directorate-General Joint Research Centre, Institute for Energy, 2007): 31, ie.jrc.ec.europa.eu/publications/scientific_publications/2007/ EUR22744EN.pdf.

7. Zaipu Tao and Mingyu Li, "What Is the Limit of Chinese Coal Supplies — A STELLA Model of Hubbert Peak," *Energy Policy* 35, Issue 6 (June 2007): 3145-3154, www.sciencedirect.com/science?_ob=ArticleURL&_udi= B6V2W-4MT59CW-2&_user=10&_rdoc=1&_fmt=&_orig=search&_sort= d&view=c&_acct=C000050221&_version=1&_urlVersion=0&_userid=1 0&md5=d1a14e5e3884b3e1620c9bae7a8664c4.

8. Thomas Thielemann, Sandro Schmidt, and J. Peter Gerling , "Lignite and Hard Coal: Energy Suppliers for World Needs until the Year 2100 — An Outlook," *The International Journal of Coal Geology* 72, Issue 1 (September 2007): 1-14, sciencedirect.com/science?_ob=ArticleURL&_udi=B6V8C-4NJWNJP-2&_user= 6682544&_rdoc=1&_fmt=&_orig=search&_sort=d&view=c&_acct= C000050221&_version=1&_urlVersion=0&_userid=6682544&md5= e433f606890f77057a515cdf0330af4d.

9. Mikael Höök, Werner Zittel, Jörg Schindler, and Kjell Aleklett, "A Supply-Driven Forecast for the Future Global Coal Production," contribution to ASPO (2008): 27, tsl.uu.se/UHDSG/Publications/Coalarticle.pdf.

10. David B. Rutledge, "Hubbert's Peak, the Coal Question, and Climate Change," California Institute of Technology, presentation (2007), rutledge.caltech.edu.

11. Jean Laherrère, "Combustibles Fossiles: Quel Avenir pour Quel Monde?" *Association pour l'étude des pics de production de pétrole et de gaz natural,* aspofrance.viabloga.com/files/JL-Versailles-long.pdf.

12. Quoted in Jim Bai, "China Needs to Cut Energy Reliance on Coal — Official," *Reuters UK,* February 4, 2008, uk.reuters.com/article/oilRpt/ idUKPEK13357320080204.

CHAPTER 4

1. Rosinformugol, *History of Coal Industry of Russia,* rosugol.ru/eng/his/index.html.

2. Mikael Höök, Werner Zittel, Jörg Schindler, and Kjell Aleklett, "A Supply-Driven Forecast for the Future Global Coal Production," contribution to ASPO (2008): 23, tsl.uu.se/UHDSG/Publications/Coalarticle.pdf.

3. eia.doe.gov/emeu/international/RecentPrimaryCoalProductionMST.xls

4. "Russia Coal Exports to Start Falling," *Reuters,* June 6, 2007, reuters.com/article/GlobalEnergy07/idUSL0638050320070606.

5. BP, *Statistical Review of World Energy 2008* (BP, June 2008), 32, bp.com/productlanding.do?categoryId=6929&contentId=7044622.

6. World Energy Council, *Survey of Energy Reserves 2007* (WEC, September 2007), Table 1.1, "Coal: Proved Recoverable Reserves at End 2005," worldenergy.org/documents/coal_1_1.pdf.

7. A. Salamatin, "Coal Industry of Russia — The State of the Art and Prospects for Development," *Mining for Tomorrow's World* (Düsseldorf, Germany, 8-10 June 1999, Bonn, Germany: Wirtschaftsvereinigung Bergbau e.V., 1999), 329-335.

8. Werner Zittel and Jörg Schindler, "Coal: Resources and Future Production," *EWG-Series No. 1/2007,* Energy Watch Group, (2007): 16, energywatchgroup.org/fileadmin/global/pdf/EWG_Report_Coal_10-07-2007ms.pdf.

9. B. Kavalov and S.D. Peteves, *The Future of Coal* (Luxembourg: European Commission, Directorate-General Joint Research Centre, Institute for Energy, 2007), 33, ie.jrc.ec.europa.eu/publications/scientific_publications/2007/EUR22744EN.pdf.

10. Thomas Thielemann, Sandro Schmidt, and J. Peter Gerling , "Lignite and Hard Coal: Energy Suppliers for World Needs until the Year 2100 — An Outlook," *The International Journal of Coal Geology* 72 (Issue 1, September 2007): 1-14, sciencedirect.com/science?_ob=ArticleURL&_udi=B6V8C-4NJWNJP-2&_user=6682544&_rdoc=1&_fmt=&_orig=search&_sort=d&view=c&_acct=C000050221&_version=1&_urlVersion=0&_userid=6682544&md5=e433f606890f77057a515cdf0330af4d).

11. Mikael Höök, Werner Zittel, Jörg Schindler, and Kjell Aleklett, "A Supply-Driven Forecast for the Future Global Coal Production," contribution to ASPO (2008): 23-25, tsl.uu.se/UHDSG/Publications/Coalarticle.pdf.

12. David B. Rutledge, "Hubbert's Peak, the Coal Question, and Climate Change," California Institute of Technology, presentation (2007), rutledge.caltech.edu.

13. Jackie Cowhig and Simon Shuster, "Russia Hydro, Rail Shortage to Cut Coal Exports," *Reuters India,* July 8, 2008, in.reuters.com/article/oilRpt/idINB65731720080707.

14. The Economist, "Trouble in the Pipeline," *The Economist,* May 8 2008, economist.com/business/displaystory.cfm?story_id=11332313.

15. World Coal Institute, "India," worldcoal.org/pages/content/index.asp?PageID=402.

16. Heading Out, post on "From ASPO-USA to MinExpo — A Study in Contrasts," The Oil Drum, comment posted September 30, 2008, theoildrum.com/node/4579.

17. "Dedicated Freight Corridor Is Answer to Coal Woes," an interview with Mr. Partha S. Bhattacharyya, Chairman of Coal India, *The Hindu Business Line,* June 30, 2008, thehindubusinessline.com/2008/06/30/stories/2008063050311400.htm.

18. Gordon Couch, "Clean Coal Technology Developments in India," (Network for Oil and Gas seminar held in Stockholm, June 14, 2007): 7-8, nog.se/files/NOG-referat_%20070614.pdf.

19. World Coal Institute, "India," worldcoal.org/pages/content/index.asp?PageID=402.

20. Sanjay Dutta, "Coal Shortage to Fuel Power Crisis," *The Times of India*, May 8, 2008, timesofindia.indiatimes.com/Business/India_Business/Coal_shortage_to_fuel_power_crisis/articleshow/3019788.cms.

21. Werner Zittel and Jörg Schindler, "Coal: Resources and Future Production," *EWG-Series No. 1/2007*, Energy Watch Group, (2007): 5, energywatchgroup.org/fileadmin/global/pdf/EWG_Report_Coal_10-07-2007ms.pdf.

22. Ibid., 11.

23. B. Kavalov and S.D. Peteves, *The Future of Coal* (Luxembourg: European Commission, Directorate-General Joint Research Centre, Institute for Energy, 2007), 34-35, ie.jrc.ec.europa.eu/publications/scientific_publications/2007/EUR22744EN.pdf.

24. Thomas Thielemann, Sandro Schmidt, and J. Peter Gerling , "Lignite and Hard Coal: Energy Suppliers for World Needs until the Year 2100 — An Outlook," *The International Journal of Coal Geology* 72 (Issue 1, September 2007): 1-14, sciencedirect.com/science?_ob=ArticleURL&_udi=B6V8C-4NJWNJP-2&_user=6682544&_rdoc=1&_fmt=&_orig=search&_sort=d&view=c&_acct=C000050221&_version=1&_urlVersion=0&_userid=6682544&md5=e433f606890f77057a515cdf0330af4d).

25. Mikael Höök, Werner Zittel, Jörg Schindler, and Kjell Aleklett, "A Supply-Driven Forecast for the Future Global Coal Production," contribution to ASPO (2008): 27-28, tsl.uu.se/UHDSG/Publications/Coalarticle.pdf.

26. David B. Rutledge, "Hubbert's Peak, the Coal Question, and Climate Change," California Institute of Technology, presentation (2007), rutledge.caltech.edu/.

CHAPTER 5

1. Mikael Höök, Werner Zittel, Jörg Schindler, and Kjell Aleklett, "A Supply-Driven Forecast for the Future Global Coal Production," contribution to ASPO (2008): 29, tsl.uu.se/UHDSG/Publications/Coalarticle.pdf.

2. Australian Coal Association, "Australia's Black Coal Exports by Destination: 2006-07," ACA, australiancoal.com.au/exports0607.htm.

3. Mikael Höök, Werner Zittel, Jörg Schindler, and Kjell Aleklett, "A Supply-Driven Forecast for the Future Global Coal Production," contribution to ASPO (2008): 29, tsl.uu.se/UHDSG/Publications/Coalarticle.pdf.

4. Australian Coal Association, "Coal through History," ACA, australiancoal.com.au/history.htm.

5. Mikael Höök, Werner Zittel, Jörg Schindler, and Kjell Aleklett, "A Supply-Driven Forecast for the Future Global Coal Production," contribution to ASPO (2008): 29, tsl.uu.se/UHDSG/Publications/Coalarticle.pdf.

6. Werner Zittel and Jörg Schindler, "Coal: Resources and Future Production," *EWG-Series No. 1/2007*, Energy Watch Group, (2007): 21,

energywatchgroup.org/fileadmin/global/pdf/EWG_Report_Coal_
10-07-2007ms.pdf.

7. B. Kavalov and S.D. Peteves, *The Future of Coal* (Luxembourg: European
Commission, Directorate-General Joint Research Centre, Institute for Energy,
2007), 26-28, ie.jrc.ec.europa.eu/publications/scientific_publications/2007/
EUR22744EN.pdf.

8. Thomas Thielemann, Sandro Schmidt, and J. Peter Gerling , "Lignite and Hard
Coal: Energy Suppliers for World Needs until the Year 2100 — An Outlook,"
The International Journal of Coal Geology 72 (Issue 1, September 2007): 1-14,
sciencedirect.com/science?_ob=ArticleURL&_udi=B6V8C-4NJWNJP-2&_
user=6682544&_rdoc=1&_fmt=&_orig=search&_sort=d&view=c&_acct=
C000050221&_version=1&_urlVersion=0&_userid=6682544&md5=
e433f606890f77057a515cdf0330af4d).

9. Mikael Höök, Werner Zittel, Jörg Schindler, and Kjell Aleklett, "A Supply-
Driven Forecast for the Future Global Coal Production," contribution to ASPO
(2008): 29, tsl.uu.se/UHDSG/Publications/Coalarticle.pdf.

10. David B. Rutledge, "Hubbert's Peak, the Coal Question, and Climate Change,"
California Institute of Technology, presentation (2007), rutledge.caltech.edu/.

11. Mikael Höök, Werner Zittel, Jörg Schindler, and Kjell Aleklett, "A Supply-
Driven Forecast for the Future Global Coal Production," contribution to ASPO
(2008): 30, .tsl.uu.se/UHDSG/Publications/Coalarticle.pdf.

12. Ibid., 30.

13. Ibid., 30.

14. Ibid., 30.

15. BP, *Statistical Review of World Energy 2008* (BP, June 2008), bp.com/
productlanding.do?categoryId=6929&contentId=7044622.

16. B. Kavalov and S.D. Peteves, *The Future of Coal* (Luxembourg: European
Commission, Directorate-General Joint Research Centre, Institute for Energy,
2007), 28-29, ie.jrc.ec.europa.eu/publications/scientific_publications/2007/
EUR22744EN.pdf.

17. Mikael Höök, Werner Zittel, Jörg Schindler, and Kjell Aleklett, "A Supply-
Driven Forecast for the Future Global Coal Production," contribution to ASPO
(2008): 30-31, tsl.uu.se/UHDSG/Publications/Coalarticle.pdf.

18. David B. Rutledge, "Hubbert's Peak, the Coal Question, and Climate Change,"
California Institute of Technology, presentation (2007), rutledge.caltech.edu/.

19. Barbara Freese, *Coal: A Human History* (Basic Books, 2003).

20. During the British coal decline from 1970 to the present, the number of jobs in
the industry fell from 150,000 to fewer than 5,000.

21. John Maynard Keynes, *The Economic Consequences of the Peace* (New York:
Harcourt, Brace and Howe, 1920).

22. Werner Zittel and Jörg Schindler, "Coal: Resources and Future Production,"
EWG-Series No. 1/2007, Energy Watch Group, (2007): 42,
energywatchgroup.org/fileadmin/global/pdf/EWG_Report_Coal_
10-07-2007ms.pdf.

23. Celine Le Prioux, "France's Coal Mining Industry to Get Second Wind with
New Power Project," *Terra Daily,* August 20, 2006,

terradaily.com/reports/France_Coal_Mining_Industry_To_Get_Second_ Wind_With_New_Power_Project_999.html.

24. Lee B. Clarke and Alessandra McConville, *Coal in Poland* (International Energy Agency Coal Research, IEACS/01, 1998), caer.uky.edu/iea/ieacs01.shtml.

25. BP, *Statistical Review of World Energy 2008* (BP, June 2008), bp.com/productlanding.do?categoryId=6929&contentId=7044622.

26. Werner Zittel and Jörg Schindler, "Coal: Resources and Future Production," *EWG-Series No. 1/2007,* Energy Watch Group, (2007): 42, energywatchgroup.org/fileadmin/global/pdf/EWG_Report_Coal_ 10-07-2007ms.pdf.

27. BP, *Statistical Review of World Energy 2008* (BP, June 2008), 32, bp.com/productlanding.do?categoryId=6929&contentId=7044622.

28. Werner Zittel and Jörg Schindler, "Coal: Resources and Future Production," *EWG-Series No. 1/2007,* Energy Watch Group, (2007): 43, energywatchgroup.org/fileadmin/global/pdf/EWG_Report_Coal_ 10-07-2007ms.pdf.

29. B. Kavalov and S.D. Peteves, *The Future of Coal* (Luxembourg: European Commission, Directorate-General Joint Research Centre, Institute for Energy, 2007), 4 and 25, ie.jrc.ec.europa.eu/publications/scientific_publications/ 2007/EUR22744EN.pdf.

30. David B. Rutledge, "Hubbert's Peak, the Coal Question, and Climate Change," California Institute of Technology, presentation (2007), rutledge.caltech.edu/.

31. Jane Sutton, "Colombia Hopes to Boost Coal Production by 40 Pct.," *Reuters,* February 1, 2007, reuters.com/article/companyNewsAndPR/ idUSN2132846820070201.

32. World Energy Council, *Survey of Energy Reserves 2007* (WEC, September 2007), Table 1.1, "Coal: Proved recoverable reserves at end 2005," worldenergy.org/documents/coal_1_1.pdf.

33. Energy Information Administration, "Venezuela Energy Profile," tonto.eia.doe.gov/country/country_energy_data.cfm?fips=VE.

34. BP, *Statistical Review of World Energy 2008* (BP, June 2008), bp.com/productlanding.do?categoryId=6929&contentId=7044622.

35. B. Kavalov and S.D. Peteves, *The Future of Coal* (Luxembourg: European Commission, Directorate-General Joint Research Centre, Institute for Energy, 2007), 29, ie.jrc.ec.europa.eu/publications/scientific_publications/2007/ EUR22744EN.pdf.

36. Mikael Höök, Werner Zittel, Jörg Schindler, and Kjell Aleklett, "A Supply-Driven Forecast for the Future Global Coal Production," contribution to ASPO (2008): 33-34, tsl.uu.se/UHDSG/Publications/Coalarticle.pdf.

37. B. Kavalov and S.D. Peteves, *The Future of Coal* (Luxembourg: European Commission, Directorate-General Joint Research Centre, Institute for Energy, 2007), 28, ie.jrc.ec.europa.eu/publications/scientific_publications/2007/ EUR22744EN.pdf.

38. Mikael Höök, Werner Zittel, Jörg Schindler, and Kjell Aleklett, "A Supply-Driven Forecast for the Future Global Coal Production," contribution to ASPO (2008): 35, tsl.uu.se/UHDSG/Publications/Coalarticle.pdf.

39. Ibid., 32.
40. Ibid., 32.
41. Ibid., 32.
42. Ibid., 32.

CHAPTER 6

1. Thomas Thielemann, Sandro Schmidt, and J. Peter Gerling, "Lignite and Hard Coal: Energy Suppliers for World Needs until the Year 2100 — An Outlook," *The International Journal of Coal Geology* 72 (Issue 1, September 2007): 1-14, sciencedirect.com/science?_ob=ArticleURL&_udi=B6V8C-4NJWNJP-2&_user=6682544&_rdoc=1&_fmt=&_orig=search&_sort=d&view=c&_acct=C000050221&_version=1&_urlVersion=0&_userid=6682544&md5=e433f606890f77057a515cdf0330af4d.
2. J.T. Houghton et al., eds., *Climate Change 2001: Working Group 1: The Scientific Basis* (Cambridge UK: Cambridge University Press, 2001), ipcc.ch/ipccreports/assessments-reports.htm.
3. The Earth Summit, "Agenda 21, the Rio Declaration on Environment and Development, the Statement of Forest Principles, the United Nations Framework Convention on Climate Change and the United Nations Convention on Biological Diversity," (United Nations Conference on Environment and Development [UNCED], Rio de Janeiro, June 3-14, 1992), un.org/geninfo/bp/enviro.html.
4. R.T. Watson and the Core Writing Team, eds., *IPCC Third Assessment Report: Climate Change 2001: Synthesis Report* (Geneva, Switzerland: Intergovernmental Panel on Climate Change, 2001), ipcc.ch/ipccreports/assessments-reports.htm.
5. R.K. Pachauri, A. Reisinger, and the Core Writing Team, eds., *IPCC Fourth Assessment Report: Climate Change 2007* (Geneva, Switzerland: Intergovernmental Panel on Climate Change, 2008), ipcc.ch/ipccreports/assessments-reports.htm.
6. M. King Hubbert, "Energy from Fossil Fuels," *Science* 109 (February 4, 1949): 103, hubbertpeak.com/Hubbert/science1949/.
7. Colin J. Campbell and Jean Laherrère, "The End of Cheap Oil," *Scientific American* (March 1998), dieoff.org/page140.htm.
8. Robert L. Hirsch, Roger Bezdek, and Robert Wendling, *Peaking Of World Oil Production: Impacts, Mitigation, & Risk Management* (US Department of Energy, February 2005), netl.doe.gov/publications/others/pdf/oil_peaking_netl.pdf.
9. Keith Bradsher, "Fuel Subsidies Overseas Take a Toll on US," *The New York Times,* July 28, 2008, World Business, nytimes.com/2008/07/28/business/worldbusiness/28subsidy.html.
10. Andrew B. Crichton, "How Much Coal Do We Really Have? The Need for an Up-to-date Survey," *Coal Technology* (August 1948).
11. Werner Zittel and Jörg Schindler, "Peak Coal by 2025 Say Researchers," *Energy Bulletin,* Energy Watch Group, (March 28, 2007), energybulletin.net/node/28287.

12. Committee on Coal Research, Technology, and Resource Assessments to Inform Energy Policy, *Coal: Research and Development to Support National Energy Policy* (Washington DC: The National Academies Press, June 2007), nap.edu/catalog.php?record_id=11977.

13. Nebojsa Nakicenovic and Rob Swart, eds., *Special Report on Emissions Scenarios,* International Panel on Climate Change (IPCC), (Cambridge, England: Cambridge University Press, 2000), ipcc.ch/ipccreports/sres/emission/index.htm.

14. European Environment Agency, "CSI 013 Specification — Atmospheric Greenhouse Gas Concentrations," themes.eea.europa.eu/IMS/ISpecs/ISpecification20041007131717/guide_ summary_plus_public.

15. European Environment Agency, "Atmospheric Greenhouse Gas Concentrations (CSI 013) — Assessment published Apr 2008," themes.eea.europa.eu/IMS/ISpecs/ISpecification20041007131717/ IAssessment1201517963441/view_content.

16. Jean Laherrère, "Estimates of Oil Reserves," (paper presented at the EMF/IEA/IEW meeting, IIASA, Laxenburg, Austria, June 19, 2001), iiasa.ac.at/Research/ECS/IEW2001/pdffiles/Papers/Laherrère-long.pdf.

17. P.A. Kharecha and J.E. Hansen, "Implications of 'Peak Oil' for Atmospheric CO_2 and Climate," *Global Biogeochemical Cycles,* 22 (2008), pubs.giss.nasa.gov/abstracts/2008/Kharecha_Hansen.html.

18. James Hansen, "Global Warning Twenty Years Later: Tipping Points Near," columbia.edu/~jeh1/2008/TwentyYearsLater_20080623.pdf.

19. Committee on Coal Research, Technology, and Resource Assessments to Inform Energy Policy, *Coal: Research and Development to Support National Energy Policy* (Washington, DC: The National Academies Press, 2007), books.nap.edu/catalog.php?record_id=11977.

20. Kjell Aleklett, "Global Warming Exaggerated, Insufficient Oil, Natural Gas and Coal," *Energy Bulletin* (May 18, 2007), energybulletin.net/node/29845.

21. David Rutledge, "The Coal Question and Climate Change," The Oil Drum, comment posted June 25, 2007, theoildrum.com/node/2697.

22. Stephen Sitch et al., "Impacts of Future Land Cover Changes on Atmospheric CO_2 and Climate," *Global Biogeochemical Cycles* 19 (2005), agu.org/pubs/crossref/2005/2004GB002311.shtml.

23. Tsung-Hung Peng et al., "Quantification of Decadal Anthropogenic CO_2 Uptake in the Ocean Based on Dissolved Inorganic Carbon Measurements," *Nature* 396 (1998): 560-563, nature.com/nature/journal/v396/n6711/ full/396560a0.html.

24. James Hansen et al., "Target Atmospheric CO_2: Where Should Humanity Aim?" *Open Atmospheric Science Journal* 2 (2008): 217-231, bentham.org/open/toascj/openaccess2.htm.

25. Bill McKibben, *The End of Nature* (Random House, 1989), and George Monbiot, *Heat: How to Stop the Planet From Burning* (South End Press, 2007).

26. Erik Shuster, "Tracking New Coal-Fired Power Plants," National Energy Technology Laboratory, Office of Systems Analyses and Planning, (June 20, 2008), netl.doe.gov/coal/refshelf/ncp.pdf.

27. Matthew L. Wald, "Georgia Judge Cites Carbon Dioxide in Denying Coal Plant Permit," *The New York Times,* July 1, 2008, nytimes.com/2008/07/01/business/01coal.html.

28. Tim Jackson, *Material Concerns: Pollution, Profit and Quality of Life* (Routledge, 1996). For an application to environmental issues, see Larry Karp, "Global Warming and Hyperbolic Discounting," CUDARE Working Paper 934R, (Department of Agriculture & Resource Economics, UBC, July 9, 2004), repositories.cdlib.org/are_ucb/934R/..

29. Elisabeth Rosenthal, "Europe Turns Back to Coal, Raising Climate Fears," *The New York Times,* April 23, 2008, nytimes.com/2008/04/23/world/europe/23coal.html.

30. In the United States, despite the cancellation of so many new coal plants in recent years, the National Mining Association projects that about 54 percent of the nation's electric power will be coal-fired by 2030, up from the current 48 percent.

CHAPTER 7

1. National Energy Technology Lab, Department of Energy, "Clean Coal Demonstrations," netl.doe.gov/technologies/coalpower/cctc/index.html.

2. US Department of Energy, "Electricity Market Module," Report DOE/EIA-0554 (2008), (June 2008), eia.doe.gov/oiaf/aeo/assumption/pdf/electricity.pdf#page=3.

3. Dr. Elion Amit, "Public Rebuttal Testimony and Exhibits," filed on behalf of the Minnesota Department of Commerce, (October 2006), mncoalgasplant.com/puc/05-1993%20pub%20rebuttal.pdf.

4. Mark Clayton, "US Scraps Ambitious Clean-Coal Power Plant," *Christian Science Monitor,* February 1, 2008, csmonitor.com/2008/0201/p25s01-usgn.html.

5. Nuon, "Innovative Projects," nuon.com/about-nuon/Innovative-projects/magnum.jsp.

6. Iraj Isaac Rahmim, "GTL, CTL Finding Roles in Global Energy Supply," *Oil & Gas Journal* 106, no. 12 (2008), ogj.com/articles/save_screen.cfm?ARTICLE_ID=323854.

7. David Gray, "Producing Liquid Fuels from Coal," (presented at the National Research Council Board on Energy and Environmental Systems Workshop on Trends in Oil Supply and Demand, Washington DC, October 20-21, 2005), 7. nationalacademies.org/bees/David_Gray_Coal_to_Liquids.pdf.

8. Dave Montgomery, "Liquefied-coal Industry Gains Energy," *McClatchy Newspapers,* August 22, 2008, mcclatchydc.com/260/story/50010.html.

9. Mike Schaefer, "The World's Biggest Investors Moving into CTL," *Energy & Capital,* August 28, 2006, energyandcapital.com/articles/ctl-coal-energy/ 262.

10. United States Government Accountability Office Report to Congressional Requesters, "Crude Oil Uncertainty About Future Oil Supply Makes It Important to Develop a Strategy for Addressing a Peak and Decline in Oil Production," GAO-07-283, (February 2007), gao.gov/htext/d07283.html.

11. Green Car Congress, "Alter NRG Proposing Canada's First Coal-to-Liquids Project," article posted July 23, 2008, greencarcongress.com/ coaltoliquids_ctl/index.html.

12. "Coal-to-Liquids — West Virginia Ready to Become a Global Leader," *Bluefield Daily Telegraph,* July 30, 2008, bdtonline.com/editorials/local_ story_212160804.html.

13. DKRW Advanced Fuels, "Medicine Bow Fuel & Power LLC," dkrwaf.com/fw/main/Medicine-Bow-111.html.

14. William Siemens, *Transactions of the Chemical Society* 21, No. 279 (1868).

15. The World Energy Council, *Underground Coal Gasification* (London: World Energy Council Survey of Energy Resources 2007), worldenergy.org/publications/survey_of_energy_resources_2007/coal/634.asp.

16. Bert Metz et al., eds., *Carbon Dioxide Capture and Storage,* International Panel on Climate Change (IPCC), (Cambridge, England: Cambridge University Press, 2005), ipcc.ch/ipccreports/srccs.htm.

17. Joint Statement by G-8 Energy Ministers, Aomori, Japan, June 8, 2008, enecho.meti.go.jp/topics/g8/g8sta_eng.pdf.

18. Bert Metz et al., eds., *Carbon Dioxide Capture and Storage,* International Panel on Climate Change (IPCC), (Cambridge, England: Cambridge University Press, 2005), ipcc.ch/ipccreports/srccs.htm.

19. United States Government Accountability Office, Report to Congressional Requesters, *Key Challenges Remain for Developing and Deploying Advanced Energy Technologies to Meet Future Needs* (Department of Energy, December 2006), gao.gov/new.items/d07106.pdf.

20. Ibid.

21. Richard Bell, "Wanna Bet the Farm on Carbon Capture and Sequestration?" comment posted on Global Public Media, April 17, 2007, globalpublicmedia.com/richard_bell_wanna_bet_the_farm_on_carbon_ capture_and_sequestration.

22. Energy Information Administration, *World Energy Overview: 1995-2005* (EIA, Report Released June-October 2007), eia.doe.gov/iea/overview.html.

23. Mining Journal Online, "Mining Explained," mining-journal.com/html/Mining_ Explained.html.

24. Climate Change Institute, "Human Impacts on the Landscape," The University of Maine, climatechange.umaine.edu/Research/Contrib/ html/22.html.

25. James Katzner et al., "The Future of Coal: Options for a Carbon-Constrained World," Massachusetts Institute of Technology, March 2007. web.mit.edu/coal/The_Future_of_Coal.pdf.

26. Vaclav Smil, "Long-range Energy Forecasts Are No More Than Fairy Tales," *Nature* 453, No. 154 (May 8, 2008, Correspondence), nature.com/nature/journal/v453/n7192/full/453154a.html.

Chapter 8

1. Committee on Coal Research, Technology, and Resource Assessments to Inform Energy Policy, *Coal: Research and Development to Support National Energy Policy* (Washington DC: The National Academies Press, 2007), nap.edu/catalog.php?record_id=11977.

2. Nicholas Stern, *The Economics of Climate Change: The Stern Review* (Cambridge, England: Cambridge University Press, 2007), and Intergovernmental Panel on

Climate Change, *Climate Change 2007 — Mitigation of Climate Change: Working Group III contribution to the Fourth Assessment* (Cambridge, England: Cambridge University Press, 2007).

3. Ted Trainer, "A Short Critique of the Stern Review," *Real-World Economics Review,* 45 (March 15, 2008): 54-58, mindfully.org/Air/2008/Stern-Review-Trainer15mar08.htm.

4. High Plains/Midwest Ag Journal, "Energy Balance of Corn-Based Ethanol Even More Favorable Than Early Estimates," October 3, 2008, hpj.com/archives/2008/oct08/oct13/Energybalanceofcorn-basedet.cfm.

5. Charles Hall, "The Energy Return of (Industrial) Solar — Passive Solar, PV, Wind and Hydro (5 of 6)," The Oil Drum, comment posted by Nate Hagens April 29, 2008, theoildrum.com/node/3910.

6. Ted Trainer, "A Short Critique of the Stern Review," *Real-World Economics Review,* 45 (March 15, 2008): 54-58, mindfully.org/Air/2008/Stern-Review-Trainer15mar08.htm. See also: Ted Trainer, *Renewable Energy Cannot Sustain a Consumer Society* (Springer, September 26, 2007).

7. Lynn White, *The Science of Culture,* (New York: Grove Press, 1949).

8. See Adam Dadeby, "Should Eroei Be the Most Important Criterion Our Society Uses to Decide How It Meets Its Energy Needs?" The Oil Drum: Europe, comment posted August 20, 2008, europe.theoildrum.com/node/4428.

9. World Energy Council, *2007 Survey of Energy Resources,* 235.

10. Herman Daly, *Steady-State Economics* (Island Press, 1991).

11. Bill McKibben, *The End of Nature* (Random House, 1989).

Bibliography

Aleklett, Kjell. "Global Warming Exaggerated, Insufficient Oil, Natural Gas and Coal," *Energy Bulletin* (EnergyBulletin.net, May 18, 2007), energybulletin.net/node/29845.

Amit, Elion. "Public Rebuttal Testimony and Exhibits," filed on behalf of the Minnesota Department of Commerce, (October, 2006), mncoalgasplant.com/puc/05-1993%20pub%20rebuttal.pdf.

Appalachian Voices website. appvoices.org/index.php?/site/mtr_overview/.

Australian Coal Association. "Australia's Black Coal Exports by Destination: 2006-07," ACA, australiancoal.com.au/exports0607.htm.

_____. "Coal through History," ACA, australiancoal.com.au/history.htm.

Averitt, Paul. *Coal Resources of the United States* (US Geological Survey Bulletin 1412, 1975).

Bai, Jim. "China Needs to Cut Energy Reliance on Coal — Official," *Reuters UK,* February 4, 2008, uk.reuters.com/article/oilRpt/idUKPEK13357320080204.

Bell, Richard. "Wanna Bet the Farm on Carbon Capture and Sequestration?" comment posted on Global Public Media, April 17, 2007, globalpublicmedia.com/richard_bell_wanna_bet_the_farm_on_carbon_capture_and_sequestration.

Bluefield Daily Telegraph, "Coal-to-Liquids — West Virginia Ready To Become a Global Leader," July 30, 2008, bdtonline.com/editorials/local_story_212160804.html.

BP, *Statistical Review of World Energy June 2008,* (BP, June 2008), bp.com/productlanding.do?categoryId=6929&contentId=7044622.

Bradsher, Keith. "Fuel Subsidies Overseas Take a Toll on US," *The New York Times,* July 28, 2008, World Business, nytimes.com/2008/07/28/business/worldbusiness/28subsidy.html.

Cameron, Eugene N. *At the Crossroads: The Mineral Problems of the United States* (John Wiley & Sons, 1986).

Campbell, Colin J., and Jean Laherrère, "The End of Cheap Oil," *Scientific American* (March 1998), dieoff.org/page140.htm.

Campbell, Marius R. "The Value of Coal-Mine Sampling," *Economic Geology*, vol. 2, no. 1, (1907): 48-57.

Churchill, Winston S. *The World Crisis, 1911-1918,* vol. 1 (Free Press, 2005).

CIA (Central Intelligence Agency). *The World Factbook,* cia.gov/library/publications/the-world-factbook/docs/rankorderguide.html.

Clarke, Lee B., and Alessandra McConville. *Coal in Poland* (International Energy Agency Coal Research, IEACS/01, 1998), caer.uky.edu/iea/ieacs01.shtml.

Clayton, Mark. "US Scraps Ambitious Clean-Coal Power Plant," *Christian Science Monitor,* February 1, 2008, csmonitor.com/2008/0201/p25s01-usgn.html.

Cleveland, Cutler and Robert Costanza. "Energy Return on Investment (EROI)," *The Encyclopedia of Earth,* (April 2008), eoearth.org/article/Energy_return_on_investment_(EROI).

Climate Change Institute, "Human Impacts on the Landscape," The University of Maine, climatechange.umaine.edu/Research/Contrib/html/22.html.

Committee on Coal Research, Technology, and Resource Assessments to Inform Energy Policy, *Coal: Research and Development to Support National Energy Policy* (Washington, DC: The National Academies Press, 2007), books.nap.edu/catalog.php?record_id=11977.

Cornelius, Rob. "No Headwinds for Coal ... at All," *The State Journal — News for West Virginia's Leaders,* Thursday, May 8, 2008, statejournal.com/ story.cfm?func=viewstory&storyid=38327&catid=159.

Couch, Gordon. "Clean Coal Technology Developments in India," (Network for Oil and Gas seminar held in Stockholm, June 14, 2007), nog.se/files/NOG-referat_%20070614.pdf.

Cowhig, Jackie and Simon Shuster, "Russia Hydro, Rail Shortage to Cut Coal Exports," *Reuters India,* July 8, 2008, in.reuters.com/article/oilRpt/idINB65731720080707.

Crichton, Andrew B. "How Much Coal Do We Really Have? The Need for an Up-to-date Survey," *Coal Technology* (August 1948).

Dadeby, Adam. "Should EROEI Be The Most Important Criterion Our Society Uses to Decide How It Meets Its Energy Needs?" The Oil Drum: Europe, comment posted August 20, 2008, europe.theoildrum.com/node/4428.

Daly, Herman. *Steady-State Economics* (Island Press, 1991).

Deffeyes, Kenneth. *Beyond Oil: The View from Hubbert's Peak* (New York: Hill and Wang, 2005).

DKRW Advanced Fuels. "Medicine Bow Fuel & Power LLC," dkrwaf.com/fw/main/Medicine-Bow-111.html.

Dutta, Sanjay. "Coal Shortage to Fuel Power Crisis," *The Times of India,* May 8, 2008, timesofindia.indiatimes.com/Business/India_Business/Coal_shortage_ to_fuel_power_crisis/articleshow/3019788.cms.

Earth Summit, The. "Agenda 21, the Rio Declaration on Environment and Development, the Statement of Forest Principles, the United Nations Framework Convention on Climate Change and the United Nations Convention on Biological Diversity," (United Nations Conference on Environment and Development

[UNCED], Rio de Janeiro, June 3-14, 1992),
un.org/geninfo/bp/enviro.html.

Economist, The. "Trouble in the Pipeline," *The Economist,* May 8 2008,
economist.com/business/displaystory.cfm?story_id=11332313.

Energy Information Administration. *International Energy Outlook 2008,* (Official
Energy Statistics from the US Government, Report # DOE/EIA-0484, June
2008), Chapter 4, "Coal," eia.doe.gov/oiaf/ieo/coal.html.

_____. *Recoverable Coal Reserves at Producing Mines, Estimated Recoverable Reserves,
and Demonstrated Reserve Base by Mining Method* (EIA, Report DOE/EIA
0584 (2007), Report Released: September 2008),
eia.doe.gov/cneaf/coal/page/acr/table15.html.

_____. "Venezuela Energy Profile," tonto.eia.doe.gov/country/country_energy_
data.cfm?fips=VE.

_____. *World Energy Overview: 1995-2005* (EIA, Report, Released June-October 2007),
eia.doe.gov/iea/overview.html.

European Environment Agency. "CSI 013 Specification — Atmospheric Greenhouse
Gas Concentrations," themes.eea.europa.eu/IMS/ISpecs/
ISpecification20041007131717/guide_summary_plus_public.

Freese, Barbara. *Coal: A Human History* (Basic Books, 2003).

Gever, John, Robert Kaufmann, David Skole, and Charles Vorosmarty. *Beyond Oil: The
Threat to Food and Fuel in the Coming Decades* (Cambridge, MA: Ballinger, 1987).

Goodell, Jeff. *Big Coal: The Dirty Secret Behind America's Energy Future.* New York:
Houghton Miffllin, 2007.

Gray, David. "Producing Liquid Fuels from Coal," (presented at the National
Research Council Board on Energy and Environmental Systems Workshop on
Trends in Oil Supply and Demand, Washington DC, October 20-21, 2005),
nationalacademies.org/bees/David_Gray_Coal_to_Liquids.pdf.

Green Car Congress. "Alter NRG Proposing Canada's First Coal-to-Liquids Project,"
Coal-to-Liquids (CTL), article posted July 23, 2008,
greencarcongress.com/coaltoliquids_ctl/index.html.

Hagens, Nate. "Living for the Moment while Devaluing the Future," The Oil Drum,
comment posted June 1, 2007, theoildrum.com/node/2592.

_____. *Climate Change, Sabre Tooth Tigers, and Devaluing the Future,* The Oil Drum,
comment posted February 23, 2007, theoildrum.com/node/2243.

Hall, Charles. "The Energy Return of (Industrial) Solar — Passive Solar, PV, Wind
and Hydro (5 of 6)," The Oil Drum, comment posted by Nate Hagens April
29, 2008, theoildrum.com/node/3910.

Hansen, James. "Global Warning Twenty Years Later: Tipping Points Near," colum-
bia.edu/~jeh1/2008/TwentyYearsLater_20080623.pdf.

Hansen, J., M. Sato, P. Kharecha, D. Beerling, R. Berner, V. Masson-Delmotte, M.
Pagani, M. Raymo, D. Royer, and J. Zachos. "Target ATmospheric CO_2:
Where Should Humanity Aim?" *The Open Atmospheric Science Journal,* 2,
(2008): 217-231, bentham.org/open/toascj/openaccess2.htm.

Heading Out. post on "From ASPO-USA to MinExpo — A Study in Contrasts," The
Oil Drum, comment posted September 30, 2008,
theoildrum.com/node/4579.

Heinberg, Richard. *Coal in China,* comment posted on Global Public Media, June
27, 2008, globalpublicmedia.com/museletter_coal_in_china.

186 BLACKOUT

_____. *The Oil Depletion Protocol: A Plan to Avert Oil Wars, Terrorism, and Economic Collapse* (Gabriola Island, BC: New Society, 2006).

High Plains/Midwest Ag Journal. "Energy Balance of Corn-Based Ethanol Even More Favorable Than Early Estimates," October 3, 2008, hpj.com/archives/2008/oct08/oct13/Energybalanceofcorn-basedet.cfm.

Hindu Business Line, The. "Dedicated Freight Corridor Is Answer to Coal Woes," an interview with Mr. Partha S Bhattacharyya, Chairman of Coal India, June 30, 2008, thehindubusinessline.com/2008/06/30/stories/2008063050311400.htm.

Hirsch, Robert L., Roger Bezdek, and Robert Wendling. *Peaking Of World Oil Production: Impacts, Mitigation, & Risk Management* (US Department of Energy, February 2005), netl.doe.gov/publications/others/pdf/oil_peaking_netl.pdf.

Höök, Mikael, Werner Zittel, Jörg Schindler, and Kjell Aleklett. "A Supply-Driven Forecast for the Future Global Coal Production," contribution to ASPO (2008), tsl.uu.se/UHDSG/Publications/Coalarticle.pdf.

Houghton, J.T. et al., eds. *Climate Change 2001: Working Group 1: The Scientific Basis* (Cambridge, UK: Cambridge University Press, 2001), grida.no/publications/ other/ipcc%5Ftar/?src=/climate/ipcc_tar/wg1/index.htm.

Hubbert, M. King. "Energy from Fossil Fuels," *Science* 109 (February 4, 1949): 103, hubbertpeak.com/Hubbert/science1949/.

_____. *Techniques of Prediction as Applied to the Production of Oil and Gas, in Oil and Gas Supply Modeling,* National Bureau of Standards Special Publication 631, ed. Saul I. Gass, (Washington: National Bureau of Standards, 1982), rutledge.caltech.edu/King%20Hubbert%20Techniques%20of%20Prediction%20as%20applied%20to%20the%20production%20of%20oil%20and%20gas.pdf.

Hull, Edward. *The Coal-fields of Great Britain: Their History, Structure and Resources* (London: H. Rees, 1905).

Intergovernmental Panel on Climate Change. *Climate Change 2007 — Mitigation of Climate Change: Working Group III contribution to the Fourth Assessment* (Cambridge, England: Cambridge University Press, 2007).

International Monetary Fund. *Regional Economic Outlook: Sub-Saharan Africa* (Washington, DC: International Monetary Fund, May 2005), imf.org/external/pubs/ft/AFR/REO/2005/eng/01/pdf/ssareo.pdf.

Joint Statement by G8 Energy Ministers. Aomori, Japan, June 8, 2008, enecho.meti.go.jp/topics/g8/g8sta_eng.pdf.

Kanter, James. "International Agency Urges the Start of an 'Energy Revolution'," *The New York Times,* June 7, 2008.

Karp, Larry. "Global Warming and Hyperbolic Discounting," CUDARE Working Paper 934R, (Department of Agriculture & Resource Economics, UBC, July 9, 2004), repositories.cdlib.org/are_ucb/934R/.

Kavalov, B., and S.D. Peteves. *The Future of Coal* (Luxembourg: European Commission, Directorate-General Joint Research Centre, Institute for Energy, 2007), ie.jrc.ec.europa.eu/publications/scientific_publications/2007.php.

Keynes, John Maynard. *The Economic Consequences of the Peace* (New York: Harcourt, Brace and Howe, 1920).

Kharecha, P.A., and J.E. Hansen (2008), "Implications of 'Peak Oil' for Atmospheric CO_2 and Climate," *Global Biogeochemical Cycles* 22 (2008), pubs.giss.nasa.gov/abstracts/2008/Kharecha_Hansen.html.

Laherrère, Jean. "Combustibles Fossiles: Quel Avenir pour Quel Monde?" *Association pour l'étude des pics de production de pétrole et de gaz natural,* aspofrance.viabloga.com/files/JL-Versailles-long.pdf.

_____. "Estimates of Oil Reserves," (paper presented at the EMF/IEA/IEW meeting, IIASA, Laxenburg, Austria, June 19, 2001), iiasa.ac.at/Research/ECS/IEW2001/pdffiles/Papers/Laherrère-long.pdf.

_____. "Peak (or Plateau) of Fossil Fuels," (paper presented at Energy, Greenhouse Gases and Environment, Universidade Fernando Pessoa, Porto, Portugal 6-8 October 2008), aspofrance.viabloga.com/files/JL_Porto_long_2008.pdf.

McKibben, Bill. *The End of Nature* (Random House, 1989).

Metz, Bert et al., eds. *Carbon Dioxide Capture and Storage,* International Panel on Climate Change (IPCC), (Cambridge, England: Cambridge University Press, 2005), ipcc.ch/ipccreports/srccs.htm.

Milici, Robert C. "Production Trends of Major US Coal-Producing Regions," (in Proceedings of the International Pittsburgh Coal Conference, Pittsburgh, 1996), byronwine.com/files/coal.pdf.

Mining Journal Online. "Mining Explained," mining-journal.com/html/Mining_Explained.html.

Monbiot, George. *Heat: How to Stop the Planet From Burning* (South End Press, 2007).

Montgomery, Dave. "Liquefied-coal Industry Gains Energy," *McClatchy Newspapers,* August 22, 2008, mcclatchydc.com/260/story/50010.html.

Nakicenovic, Nebojsa, and Rob Swart, eds. *Special Report on Emissions Scenarios,* International Panel on Climate Change (IPCC), (Cambridge, England: Cambridge University Press, 2000), ipcc.ch/ipccreports/sres/emission/index.htm.

National Energy Technology Lab, Department of Energy, "Clean Coal Demonstrations," netl.doe.gov/technologies/coalpower/cctc/index.html.

National Snow and Ice Data Center, "Sea Ice Conditions at the Annual Minimum on September 16, 2007," nsidc.org/news/press/2007_seaiceminimum/20070810_index.html.

Nuon. "Innovative Projects," nuon.com/about-nuon/Innovative-projects/magnum.jsp.

OECD/International Energy Agency. *China's Power Sector Reforms: Where to Next?* (Paris: Organisation for Economic Co-operation and Development, 2006), 13, iea.org/textbase/nppdf/free/2006/chinapower.pdf.

Pachauri, R.K., A. Reisinger, and the Core Writing Team, eds. *IPCC Fourth Assessment Report: Climate Change 2007* (Geneva, Switzerland: Intergovernmental Panel on Climate Change, 2008), ipcc.ch/ipccreports/ assessments-reports.htm.

Peng, Tsung-Hung, et al. "Quantification of Decadal Anthropogenic CO_2 Uptake in the Ocean Based on Dissolved Inorganic Carbon Measurements," *Nature* 396 (1998): 560-563, nature.com/nature/journal/v396/n6711/full/396560a0.html.

Prioux, Celine Le. "France's Coal Mining Industry to Get Second Wind with New Power Project," *Terra Daily,* August 20, 2006, terradaily.com/reports/France_Coal_Mining_Industry_To_Get_Second_Wind_With_New_Power_Project_999.html.

Putnam, Palmer. *Energy in the Future* (New York: Van Nostrand, 1953).

Rahmim, Iraj Isaac. "GTL, CTL Finding Roles in Global Energy Supply," *Oil & Gas Journal* 106, no. 12 (2008), ogj.com/articles/save_screen.cfm?ARTICLE_ID=323854.

RealClimate, "Is the Ocean Carbon Sink Sinking?" article posted November 1, 2007, realclimate.org/index.php/archives/2007/11/is-the-ocean-carbon-sink-sinking/.

Reuters. "Russia Coal Exports To Start Falling," *Reuters,* June 6, 2007, reuters.com/article/GlobalEnergy07/idUSL0638050320070606.

Rice, James B. and Jill A. Janocha. "Coal Mining Injuries, Illnesses, and Fatalities in 2006," *Bureau of Labor Statistics* (June 27, 2008), bls.gov/opub/cwc/sh20080623ar01p1.htm.

Robertson, David, Angela Jameson, and Sam Coates. "Breakdowns Spark National Grid Crisis in Power Supply," *Times Online,* (September 5, 2008), business.timesonline.co.uk/tol/business/industry_sectors/utilities/article4678321.ece.

Rohrbacher, Timothy J., Dale D. Teeters, Gerald L. Sullivan, and Lee M. Osmonson. *Coal Reserves of the Matewan Quadrangle, Kentucky — A Coal Recoverability Study* (USGS, US Bureau of Mines Circular 9355), pubs.usgs.gov/usbmic/ic-9355/.

Rosenthal, Elisabeth. "Europe Turns Back to Coal, Raising Climate Fears," *The New York Times,* April 23, 2008, nytimes.com/2008/04/23/world/europe/23coal.html.

Rosinformugol, *History of Coal Industry of Russia,* rosugol.ru/eng/his/index.html.

Rutledge, David B. "Hubbert's Peak, the Coal Question, and Climate Change," California Institute of Technology, presentation (2007), rutledge.caltech.edu/.

_____. "The Coal Question and Climate Change," The Oil Drum, comment posted June 25, 2007, theoildrum.com/node/2697.

Saiget, Robert J. "China's Coal Addiction Causing Environmental Disaster," *Terra Daily,* (November 6, 2006), terradaily.com/reports/China_Coal_Addiction_Causing_Environmental_Disaster_999.html.

Salamatin, A. "Coal Industry of Russia — The State of the Art And Prospects for the Development," *Mining for Tomorrow's World* (Düsseldorf, Germany, 8-10 June 1999, Bonn, Germany: Wirtschaftsvereinigung Bergbau e.V., 1999), 329-335.

Schaefer, Mike. "The World's Biggest Investors Moving into CTL," *Energy & Capital,* August 28, 2006, energyandcapital.com/articles/ctl-coal-energy/262.

Shuster, Erik. "Tracking New Coal-Fired Power Plants," National Energy Technology Laboratory, Office of Systems Analyses and Planning, (June 20, 2008), netl.doe.gov/coal/refshelf/ncp.pdf.

Siemens, William. *Transactions of the Chemical Society* 21, No. 279 (1868).

Sitch, S., et al. "Impacts of Future Land Cover Changes on Atmospheric CO_2 and Climate," *Global Biogeochemical Cycles* 19 (2005), agu.org/pubs/crossref/2005/2004GB002311.shtml.

Smil, Vaclav. "Long-range Energy Forecasts Are No More Than Fairy Tales," *Nature* 453, No. 154 (May 8, 2008, Correspondence), nature.com/nature/journal/v453/n7192/full/453154a.html.

Sousa, Luis de. *Olduvai Revisited 2008,* The Oil Drum: Europe, comment posted February 28, 2008, europe.theoildrum.com/node/3565.

Stern, Nicholas. *The Economics of Climate Change: The Stern Review* (Cambridge, England: Cambridge University Press, 2007).

Stradling, David and Peter Thorsheim. "The Smoke of Great Cities: British and American Efforts to Control Air Pollution, 1860-1914," *BNet* (January 1999), findarticles.com/p/articles/mi_qa3854/is_199901/ai_n8833707/pg_1.

Strahan, David. "Coal: Bleak Outlook for the Black Stuff," *New Scientist,* 2639 (2008), environment.newscientist.com/channel/earth/mg19726391.800-coal-bleak-outlook-for-the-black-stuff.html.

Sutton, Jane. "Colombia Hopes to Boost Coal Production by 40 Pct.," *Reuters,* February 1, 2007, reuters.com/article/companyNewsAndPR/idUSN2132846820070201.

Tao, Zaipu and Mingyu Li. "What is the Limit Of Chinese Coal Supplies — A STELLA Model of Hubbert Peak," *Energy Policy* 35, Issue 6 (June 2007): 3145-3154, sciencedirect.com/science?_ob=ArticleURL&_udi=B6V2W-4MT59CW-2&_user=10&_rdoc=1&_fmt=&_orig=search&_sort=d&view=c&_acct=C000050221&_version=1&_urlVersion=0&_userid=10&md5=d1a14e5e3884b3e1620c9bae7a8664c4.

Thielemann, Thomas, Sandro Schmidt, and J. Peter Gerling, "Lignite and Hard Coal: Energy Suppliers for World Needs until the Year 2100 — An Outlook," *The International Journal of Coal Geology* 72 (Issue 1, September 2007): 1-14, sciencedirect.com/science?_ob=ArticleURL&_udi=B6V8C-4NJWNJP-2&_user=6682544&_rdoc=1&_fmt=&_orig=search&_sort=d&view=c&_acct=C000050221&_version=1&_urlVersion=0&_userid=6682544&md5=e433f606890f77057a515cdf0330af4d.

Tien, Jerry C. "China's Two Major Modern Coal Projects," *Engineering and Mining Journal* (May 1, 1998).

Trainer, Ted. "A Short Critique of the Stern Review," *Real-World Economics Review,* 45, (15 March, 2008): 54-58, mindfully.org/Air/2008/Stern-Review-Trainer15mar08.htm.

US Department of Energy, "Electricity Market Module," Report DOE/EIA-0554 (2008), (June 2008), eia.doe.gov/oiaf/aeo/assumption/pdf/electricity.pdf#page=3.

US Geological Survey, *National Coal Resource Assessment (NCRA),* energy.cr.usgs.gov/coal/coal_assessments/summary.html.

US Government Accountability Office. Report to Congressional Requesters. "Crude Oil Uncertainty about Future Oil Supply Makes It Important to Develop a Strategy for Addressing a Peak and Decline in Oil Production," GAO-07-283, (February 2007), gao.gov/htext/d07283.html.

_____. Report to Congressional Requesters, *Key Challenges Remain for Developing and Deploying Advanced Energy Technologies to Meet Future Needs* (Department of Energy, December 2006), gao.gov/new.items/d07106.pdf.

Vernon, Chris. *Climate Change — An Alternative Approach,* The Oil Drum: Europe, comment posted November 21, 2007, theoildrum.com/node/3263.

_____. *Dr. James Hansen: Can We Still Avoid Dangerous Human-Made Climate Change?* The Oil Drum: Europe, comment posted November 22, 2006, europe.theoildrum.com/story/2006/11/18/93514/869.

_____. *Implications of "Peak Oil" for Atmospheric CO_2 and Climate,* The Oil Drum: Europe, comment posted May 22, 2007, europe.theoildrum.com/node/2559#more.

_____. *More Coal Equals More CO_2,* The Oil Drum: Europe, comment posted October 22, 2006, europe.theoildrum.com/story/2006/10/16/184756/92.

_____. *Peak Oil and Climate Change,* The Oil Drum: Europe, comment posted January 21, 2007, europe.theoildrum.com/node/2200.

Vidal, John. "Global Food Crisis Looms as Climate Change and Fuel Shortages Bite," *The Guardian*, November 3, 2007, guardian.co.uk/environment/2007/nov/03/food.climatechange.

Wald, Matthew L. "Georgia Judge Cites Carbon Dioxide in Denying Coal Plant Permit," *The New York Times*, July 1, 2008, nytimes.com/2008/07/01/business/01coal.html.

Watson, R.T. and the Core Writing Team, eds. *IPCC Third Assessment Report: Climate Change 2001: Synthesis Report* (Geneva, Switzerland: Intergovernmental Panel on Climate Change, 2001), ipcc.ch/ipccreports/assessments-reports.htm.

White, Lynn. *The Science of Culture* (New York: Grove Press, 1949).

Wood Jr., Gordon H., Thomas M. Kehn, M. Devereux Carter, and William C. Culbertson. "Coal Resource Classification System of the US Geological Survey," *Geological Survey Circular 891*, USGS, pubs.usgs.gov/circ/c891/.

World Coal Institute. "Coal Transportation," worldcoal.org/pages/content/index.asp?PageID=93.

_____. "India," worldcoal.org/pages/content/index.asp?PageID=402.

World Energy Council. *2004 Survey of Energy Resources*, (London: World Energy Council, 2004), worldenergy.org/documents/ser2004.pdf.

_____. *Survey of Energy Reserves 2007* (London: World Energy Council, September 2007), worldenergy.org/documents/coal_1_1.pdf.

_____. *Underground Coal Gasification* (London: World Energy Council Survey of Energy Resources 2007), worldenergy.org/publications/survey_of_energy_resources_2007/coal/634.asp.

Wright, Tim. "Growth of the Modern Chinese Coal Industry: An Analysis of Supply and Demand, 1896-1936," *Modern China 7* (1981): 317-350, mcx.sagepub.com/cgi/reprint/7/3/317.

Zittel, Werner and Jörg Schindler. "Coal: Resources and Future Production," *EWG-Series No. 1/2007*, Energy Watch Group, (2007), energywatchgroup.org/fileadmin/global/pdf/EWG_Report_Coal_10-07-2007ms.pdf.

_____. "Peak Coal by 2025 Say Researchers," *Energy Bulletin*, Energy Watch Group (March 28, 2007), energybulletin.net/node/28287.

Index

About the Author

Richard Heinberg is the author of nine books including Gold IPPY award winner, *Peak Everything,* and is the senior Fellow of the Post Carbon Institute. His scores of published articles touch on the most important aspects of the human condition, always with a view to the historical and cultural context of our unique moment in time. A recipient of the M. King Hubbert Award for Excellence in Energy Education, Heinberg lectures widely on oil depletion and its implications for agriculture, urban planning, and daily life. See also RichardHeinberg.com.

If you have enjoyed *Blackout* you might also enjoy other

Books to Build a New Society

Our books provide positive solutions for people who want
to make a difference. We specialize in:

Sustainable Living • Green Building • Peak Oil • Renewable Energy
Environment & Economy • Natural Building & Appropriate Technology
Progressive Leadership • Resistance and Community
Educational and Parenting Resources

New Society Publishers

ENVIRONMENTAL BENEFITS STATEMENT

New Society Publishers has chosen to produce this book on Enviro 100, recycled paper made with **100% post consumer waste**, processed chlorine free, and old growth free.

For every 5,000 books printed, New Society saves the following resources:[1]

21	Trees
1,911	Pounds of Solid Waste
2,103	Gallons of Water
2,742	Kilowatt Hours of Electricity
3,474	Pounds of Greenhouse Gases
15	Pounds of HAPs, VOCs, and AOX Combined
5	Cubic Yards of Landfill Space

[1]Environmental benefits are calculated based on research done by the Environmental Defense Fund and other members of the Paper Task Force who study the environmental impacts of the paper industry.

For a full list of NSP's titles, please call **1-800-567-6772** *or check out our website at:*

www.newsociety.com

NEW SOCIETY PUBLISHERS